JAPAN

Edited by Simon Holledge
Introduction by Murray Sayle

Text by Simon Holledge, Alan Booth, Robert David Jack, James K Weatherly
and Patricia Yamada

Contributions by Hamish McDonald,
Michael Gorman, Murray Sayle and Glenda Bendure

Photographs
by The Stockhouse

MPC

Torii gate, Miyajima

© Odyssey Production Ltd 1988

Published by CFW Publications Ltd.
1602 Alliance Bldg
130 Connaught Rd C
Hong Kong

Published in the UK and Europe by
Moorland Publishing Co Ltd,
Moor Farm Road, Airfield Estate,
Ashbourne, Derbyshire,
DE6 1HD, England

Printed by Yee Tin Tong Printing Press Ltd.
Tong Chong Street,
Quarry Bay,
Hong Kong.

Produced by Odyssey Productions Ltd.

Acknowledgements

Text: Simon Holledge (Visiting Japan, The Tokyo Region, Northeast Honshu, Appendices); Alan Booth (The Islands of Kyushu and Hokkaido, Niigata, Hiroshima, Hagi, Matsue, Amanohashidate); Robert David Jack (Ise, Nara, Osaka); James K Weatherly (The Island of Shikoku, Kanazawa, Japan Alps, Takayama, Himeji); Patricia Yamada (Kyoto, Noto Peninsula).
Contributions: Hamish McDonald (Nagoya, Okinawa); Michael Gorman (Okayama City); Murray Sayle (Mount Fuji); Glenda Bendure (Kobe).

ISBN 0 86190 214 9   Printed in Hong Kong.

Contents

Introduction by Murray Sayle 7
    The Periods of Japanese History 13
Visiting Japan 15
    When to Go 15
    What to Pack 16
    Visa and Health Requirements 17
    Customs 17
    Tourist Information Services, Tours and Guides 17
    Transport 20
    International Communications 24
    English-language Media 24
    Money 25
    Shopping 25
    Outdoor Sport and Recreation 29
    The Arts, Entertainment and Nightlife 33
    Festivals 37
Destinations
    Tokyo Region (Kanto) 39
    Yokohama 52
    Kamakura 52
    Hakone 54
    Nikko 54
    Mashiko 57
    Northeast Honshu (Tohoku) 57
    Sendai and Matsushima 58
    Aizu Basin and Mount Bandai 60
    Hiraizumi 61
    Rikuchu Coast 61
    Morioka 63
    Hachimantai Plateau, Lake Tazawa and Lake Towada 63
    Hirosaki and Tsugaru Peninsula 64
    Mount Osore and Shimokita Peninsula 64
    Central Honshu (Chubu) 65
    Mount Fuji 68
    Nagoya and the Pacific Coast 68
    Kanazawa 71
    Noto Peninsula and Wajima 72
    Niigata and Sado Island 72
    Japan Alps 73
    Takayama 75
    Kyoto, Nara and Osaka Region (Kinki) 75

Ise	77
Nara	78
Kyoto	83
Osaka	88
Kobe	90
Himeji	92
Amanohashidate	92
Western Honshu (Chugoku)	93
Okayama City and Kurashiki	93
Hiroshima and Miyajima	95
Hagi	97
Matsue and Izumo	97
Shikoku Island	100
Takamatsu	101
Tokushima	101
Kochi	101
Matsuyama	103
Kyushu Island	103
Nagasaki	103
Kumamoto and Mount Aso	105
Kagoshima and Sakurajima	108
Miyazaki and Mount Kirishima	109
Beppu	110
Okinawa	111
Hokkaido Island	112
Sapporo	114
Hakodate	114
National Parks of Hokkaido	116
Recommended Reading	120
Appendices	
Inns, Hotels and Other Accommodation	123
Eating and Drinking	130
Index	140

Introduction

For most of their history the islands of Japan have been as remote from the rest of the world, as unapproachable as Tibet is now. In Japan, geographical isolation has predictably bred social conservatism and psychological insularity, as in other out of the way places. Yet few people have ever been so intrigued by foreigners, so receptive to foreign ideas, as the Japanese. This contradiction set the great pendulum of Japanese history swinging thousands of years ago, and it swings still. At times the Japanese as a matter of deliberate policy have set out to understand and adopt useful ideas of other societies and at this they have no equal in the world, hence their reputation (widespread in China and Korea long before the Europeans came) of being imitators. Then at other periods, the Japanese have sealed themselves off from the world, most notably in the 'closed country' period of 1637 to 1868, and again, in another time of military ascendancy, from 1931 to 1945.

Since the sharp turn to the ways of peace after 1945, the last four decades have seen the greatest of all Japan's 'open country' periods taking the backward hermits of just over a century ago to the rank of third, perhaps second, industrial power in the world. On historical precedent another reaction is likely sooner or later, and there are signs, faint to be sure and possibly deceptive, that it has already begun.

Who are these people so constant in their changeableness? One of the most pernicious legacies of the 'closed country' epochs has been the doctrine, apparently confirmed by Japan's success as the only Asian and non-Christian industrial power of world rank, that the Japanese are both homogeneous and unique, and not merely different from other peoples (as we all are) but different in a more fundamental way. Most Japanese still half believe this, but a glance at the map, or at the faces opposite you in the Tokyo subway, is enough to cast doubt on the theory.

Many peoples have come to Japan, by all practicable routes, bringing more or less of their cultures to add to the final mixture. First ashore seem to have been the Ainu, hairy, swarthy people possibly of 'archaic Caucasian' stock, distant collateral relatives of Europeans. The Ainu crossed into northeastern Japan from Siberia, perhaps 20,000 years ago, perhaps earlier and came no further south than the present region of Tokyo (the name of Mount Fuji means nothing in Japanese, and is said to be derived from the Ainu verb to 'gush forth'). The Ainu never advanced beyond the Stone Age and, trading furs with the Japanese for iron weapons, hunting equipment and alcohol, were inexorably driven north. A few pure Ainu are left but the last native-born speaker of Ainu died around 1955 and their culture is effectively dead.

The Ainu contributed nothing beyond place names to Japanese civilisation, just as Queen Boadicea and King Arthur left hardly more than the word '*whisky*' to the English-speaking Anglo-Saxons. But Ainu blood is, on appearances, widespread in Japan, the more so as you go west and north. It is because of the Ainu admixture that Japanese are hairier than other Asians, and often show something indefinably European about their features. Perhaps for the same reason the women of the Japan Sea coast are said to be the most beautiful in the country.

Next to arrive, probably by way of Korea and Tsushima Island, were the Jomon people, named after a village near Tokyo. Unlike the isolated Ainu, the Jomon, who have been dated back to around 4500 BC, seem closely connected with the hunting and shell-gathering folk who once lived in an immense arc from China up through the Aleutians. They lived in pit dwellings protected by large roofs thatched with reeds not unlike those you can still see in rural Japan. On the southern island of Kyushu, they seem to have met and mingled with Malayo-Polynesians arriving by sea along the chain of islands which stretch all the way to the Philippines and beyond, scarcely ever out of sight of land. No doubt because of their Polynesian heritage, the people of southwestern Japan are on the whole slighter, darker in colouring, and famous for their fiery tempers.

The Stone Age ended with the landing of the Yayoi people around the 2nd century BC, probably from Korea (and according to legend in stone boats). The Yayoi are the great unsolved mystery of Japanese history, but whoever they were they were fast workers. In Japan's first crash programme of modernisation, the Yayoi brought rice culture, then bronze (a technique learnt from China though the Yayoi were certainly not Chinese), and then the iron swords which have fascinated Japanese ever since. In a few generations, Japan covered a cultural distance which had taken other peoples thousands, tens of thousands of years to achieve.

Why? Like most historical riddles, the answer to this one is probably necessity. Japanese geography has changed little, fundamentally, since the time of the Yayoi. The islands (other than Hokkaido in the north) have granite spines seamed with steep, narrow valleys. Earthquakes are frequent, and so are typhoons. Even more destructive, they can turn the rocky watercourses into raging torrents in a few hours. A man alone has little chance against these natural disasters. Nor is Japan, which alternates a Siberian winter with a short humid summer, naturally endowed to grow rice, cotton and tea, crops which originated in the tropics.

To survive above the precarious level of hunting, Japanese were obliged to work together in clans, for which the valleys provided natural frames. In return for total loyalty, the clan offered comparative security in times of calamity. Rivalry between the clans led to an active search for and ready acceptance of new technology, agricultural and military, and the passionate attachment of every warrior and farmer to the interests of his group. Many of these attitudes can still be seen to this day in the relationship of the Japanese employee to his company.

The Yayoi people seem to have come in waves, impelled no doubt by events in Korea and on the Asian mainland. With one such immigration came the basic structure of the Japanese language, which is *not* unique (Ainu has a much better claim) but belongs to the western Mongolian group. Korean is also a member of this broad language family, but as a part of the eastern group, is only a distant relative of Japanese. This explains the dissimilarity of the neighbouring languages, and the unfounded view that Japanese is unconnected with other tongues. We can also dimly perceive the arrival in Japan, at some time close to the beginning of the Christian era, of a body of horse-riding nomads from central Asia, armed with steel weapons and bringing with them the shamanistic religion with its bright colours, bells and drums, which later coalesced with older animistic beliefs to form *Shinto* (Way of the Gods), Japan's still flourishing folk religion.

Much light is being thrown on Japanese prehistory by linguistic and archaeological studies, discouraged in Japan before 1945 and by the Japanese when they ruled Korea, which are now actively proceeding in both countries. This reluctance, in the past, was partly to protect from scientific scrutiny the legends surrounding the origins of the Japanese people and, more particularly, those of Japan's nameless and undoubtedly very ancient imperial family. The family seems to have emerged in late Yayoi times as hereditary chiefs of the clan residing in the region called Yamato which settled in the plain which was to be the site of the future capital cities Nara and Kyoto, and of today's bustling commercial megapolis Osaka.

The ruling family of Yamato had already established some sort of hegemony over the tribes of Kyushu and most of Honshu when Japanese history steps into the light of literacy, with the introduction of Buddhism into Japan in, or close to, 552 at a time when the Yamato clan also ruled part of south Korea (or was possibly itself controlled from there). With Buddhism, the only universal idea ever to take firm root in Japan, came Chinese script, which was in turn the vehicle for the immense body of Chinese thought and literature (the vocabulary of modern Japanese is more than half Chinese in origin, although English words are these days pouring into the language like the Chinese which preceded it). Although Chinese writings came to Japan, few Chinese or any other foreigners did. Even fewer settled. So apart from today's half-million-strong, ill-assimilated Korean minority, the Japanese of the 5th century are pretty much the Japanese of the 20th century. Not surprisingly, they are one of the world's more inward-looking clannish people: paradoxically the one most dependent on trade with foreigners for survival.

The subsequent course of Japanese history is reflected in the movements of the capital. Until 794 it was at Nara, some of whose ancient glories still survive. Then, under the influence of Chinese geomancy, it was moved to a site with the desirable setting of a mountain to the north, sea to the east and a river to the west. It was at first called Heian, then simply Kyoto (Capital). In 1192, after decades of civil war, the warrior Minamoto Yoritomo (1147-1199), assuming the title of Barbarian-quelling Generalissimo (Seii-tai-shogun or Shogun for short), set up a military regime headquartered at Kamakura, near modern Tokyo, and instituted the system of rule by hereditary ministers which lasted until 1868.

The shogunate passed, usually violently, from one family to another to come to rest finally with the military clan named Tokugawa. The founder, Ieyasu (1542-1616), who was proclaimed shogun in 1603, left many reminders of his time. His mausoleum at Nikko is one of the most-visited sites in Japan. The immense city of Tokyo (Eastern Capital) was formerly Edo, the castle town of the Tokugawa, and the Emperor of Japan resides in what was once the Tokugawa fortress. But modern Japan itself, with its passion for education, its powerful bureaucracy and disciplined citizens, is really the most durable monument of the Tokugawa.

The last Tokugawa shogun was deposed by a coalition of military men, members of the class of hereditary warriors, the samurai. In theory, Emperor Meiji was 'restored' to rule in 1868, but in practice power was exercised by the people who had overthrown the shogun. Ironically, one of their first reforms was to abolish the privileges of the samurai class in 1874. This included their treasured right to wear two swords, with which they could formerly strike off the heads of common people who showed them less than fitting respect. With the Meiji Restoration came Japan's frantic rush to catch up with the outside world, at first aimed at achieving military strength so that the world could still be kept at arms' length, and then, when Japan's military adventures ended in disaster in 1945, to provide an ever more comfortable life for the Japanese people. The success of the modernisation drive, unique in Asia, astonished even the Japanese, especially those who had forgotten the historical lesson that Japan had already done the same thing once before in absorbing the achievements of China.

The visitor to today's Japan will thus find great uniformity, unexpected variety, and hardly ever what he or she expects. The centres of the big Japanese cities all look much the same as most of them were burnt out during the Second World War and rebuilt in a mixture of western architectural styles so bizarre that it has become a style in itself.

This is high technology, luxury Japan, where the rents of western-sized apartments and the price of steak and wine infallibly put Tokyo top of the list of the world's most expensive cities. Beyond stretch the suburbs, where few foreigners ever go, the true Japanese wilderness of box-like, primitively-sewered houses, *pachinko* (Japanese pinball) parlours and inhumanly crowded railway stations ringed by jungles of rusty bicycles. Beyond that the zone (diminishing every year) of exquisite, garden-like Japanese farms, the source of the cities' moral values, and the fondly-remembered home villages of most of the cities' hyper-active inhabitants. Beyond that again the blue on grey of the mountains, in Japan never completely out of sight.

In a short train journey we can go forward, or back, several centuries. On the same ticket we see the arctic meet the tropics, with ice lacing bamboo groves, and wild monkeys scampering through snowy pine forests. North to south, or east to west as Japanese think of their country lying, Japan is in life-style strikingly, even monotonously uniform, in geography very varied.

Hokkaido, the northernmost island, is ecologically an extension of Siberia. It was only settled by substantial numbers of Japanese in the late 19th century, and is thus the last surviving example of a Japanese colony. The island has comparatively broad plains which skirt the central mountain core, hardly any secluded valleys, and long, straight roads lined with birch trees. The farms are big by Japanese standards, with Dutch barns and silos for cattle fodder. Hokkaido people have a pioneering hardiness and egalitarian spirit, but they speak Tokyo dialect, and the capital city, Sapporo, is as sophisticated as any fashionable Tokyoite could wish and considerably more affordable.

Honshu, which means simply 'Mainland', has around Tokyo and the south some of the most congested industrial areas in the world, also Japan's highest mountains (overtopped of course by the incomparable Fuji), and Tohoku, the north or east, where fishing villages cling to clefts in the cliffs and the villagers every winter build barriers of driftwood to protect their houses from the pitiless winds whipping off the sea. These latter Japanese have a streak of steel in them, far removed from the cherry blossoms and paper lanterns of the tourist posters. At the other end of Honshu is the martyred city of Hiroshima, now completely rebuilt and thriving, and the island-studded Inland Sea, an inexhaustible subject for photography.

Kyushu is Japan's deep south, with palm trees and immense groves of mandarin oranges, yet another valuable Japanese import from China. Kyushu has many semi-active volcanoes. One of them, Sakurajima, regularly rains ash on the historic bayside city of Kagoshima. It suffers more than the rest of Japan from typhoons but is otherwise a peaceful island. Even quieter is Shikoku, island of Buddhist temples, a combined version in miniature of the other three. Between and beyond the main four there are islands by the thousands, ranging in size from Sado, once the home of an exiled emperor, down to picturesque rocks, the home of seals and seabirds. Every year, another small island lived on for centuries is abandoned, its hardy inhabitants lured away by the bright lights and factory jobs of the big Japanese cities.

The pace of change of Japanese life has never been faster than it is now, so that the perceptions of twenty and even ten years ago are already out of date. The Japanese poor are no longer poor by European standards and the once-polluted cities now have some of the cleanest urban air in the world. The new Japanese middle-class, or rather universal class, is beginning to talk about how to fill in leisure time, a problem which concerned only a handful of aristocratic Kyoto families as recently as a century ago. The day may not be far distant when electronic robots will do most of Japan's work and the Japanese can all live like Heian courtiers.

The Periods of Japanese History

Jomon	c. 4500 BC — c. 200 BC
Yayoi	c. 200 BC — c. 250 AD
Kofun (Tumulus)	c. 250 — 552
Asuka	552 — 645
Early Nara (Hakuho)	645 — 710
Late Nara (Tempyo)	710 — 794
Early Heian (Konin)	794 — 898
Late Heian (Fujiwara)	898 — 1185
Kamakura	1185 — 1333
Northern and Southern Courts	1336 — 1392
Ashikaga (Muromachi)	1392 — 1573
Momoyama (Azuchi-Momoyama)	1573 — 1603
Tokugawa (Edo)	1603 — 1868
Modern: Meiji Era	1868 — 1912
Taisho Era	1912 — 1926
Showa Era	1926 —

Note Throughout this book the names of Japanese people are given in the orthodox Japanese style, with the surname before the personal name.

VISITING JAPAN

The Japanese offer great hospitality to foreign visitors. There are few places in the world where the people are so responsive to the demands of strangers. And yet it is a different society with different values, different ways of doing things. Facilities available for travellers are almost without exception designed for the Japanese themselves, not for foreign tourists. The domestic travel industry dwarfs its international counterpart.

During the 1970s the travel establishment assumed that all foreigners had come to Japan to see the great historical sights, and perhaps climb Mount Fuji. Accommodated in Tokyo and Kyoto, few tourists went further afield than a day excursion allowed.

Japan is being rediscovered in the 1980s. International visitors are now travelling the length and breadth of the islands, enjoying, to a much greater extent than before, the great variety of experiences that Japan has in store for its guests.

Tourists have a choice between accepting the services of professional shepherds and going it alone. The following sections are written for the benefit of both group and independent travellers.

When to Go

Guidebooks invariably recommend visitors to pick the spring or autumn to come to Japan. But the humid, temperate climate of the Japanese islands is far less predictable than that of the Asian continent, and this advice has to be qualified.

Spring is generally fine and relatively dry; the cherry blossoms that open in the island of Kyushu in March spread up to the north of Honshu by the beginning of May. They do not bloom in the same place at exactly the same time each year.

Early summer is often the wettest season of the year. Late summer is normally very hot and humid, only relieved by occasional typhoons arriving from the south. August is the hottest month of the year, and is an uncomfortable time to be touring the sights around Tokyo and Kyoto. On the other hand it is a great time to be in the mountains of central and northeastern Honshu and on the island of Hokkaido. Late summer is the best time to see Japan's wonderful alpine flora.

The colours of a Japanese autumn are as fine as those anywhere else in the world. This is the driest time of the year for most of the country south and west of the Japan Alps. November is the finest season in Kyoto.

During the winter there is thick snow along the coastal area of Honshu facing the Japan Sea and the Asian mainland, also in northeast Honshu and Hokkaido. Skiing is very popular in all these places. Tokyo and the southern and western regions have much less snow. February is the coldest month of the year.

Temperature Chart

	Feb	May	Aug	Nov
Sapporo (Hokkaido)	-5 (23)	11 (52)	22 (72)	4 (39)
Sendai	1 (34)	14 (57)	24 (75)	8 (46)
Tokyo	4 (39)	18 (64)	26 (79)	11 (52)
Kyoto	4 (39)	18 (64)	27 (81)	11 (52)
Kagoshima (Kyushu)	8 (46)	19 (66)	27 (81)	14 (57)

(Celsius with Fahrenheit in brackets)

Travellers without comprehensive prior booking may consider avoiding the national holidays when transport and accommodation facilities are used to capacity. The most important holiday season is at New Year (December 28th to January 4th), followed by the so-called 'Golden Week' (April 29th to May 5th) and the Obon festival of the rural areas (mid August). There are interesting things for the visitor to see during New Year and Obon, but *not* during Golden Week.

What to Pack

Clothing Visitors should dress for comfort. There are still places in Tokyo that insist on formal clothing (they invariably also insist on their customers parting with a lot of money) but dress is generally much more casual than it used to be. Warm clothing, multiple layers and sometimes thermal underwear should be taken in the winter. In the summer only light cotton clothes are needed, except by mountain trekkers who will still require sweaters and anoraks.

'Slip-off' shoes are better for sightseeing than laced ones. Tourists are frequently asked to remove footwear at the entrances of historic buildings, and indeed *always* when entering Japanese-style inns and ordinary Japanese homes. Anyone staying in budget accommodation, or intending to bathe outside the hotel (for example at a hot spring) should bring a towel. On the other hand a wrap-around or dressing gown is not needed: every hotel or inn will provide a freshly washed casual light cotton kimono, called a *yukata*.

Other Items Any visitor hoping to make friends with Japanese people should bring a number of small gifts representative of his or her country, and if possible name cards. Both play an important part in Japanese social life.

The electrical current is 100 volts in Japan. American appliances will work, but a transformer will be necessary for those designed for 220 to 240 volts.

Japanese colour film is widely available but Kodak tends to be expensive and process-paid rolls are not available. Hong Kong is a better place to buy it. (Kodak processing in Tokyo and Osaka is excellent.)

Visa and Health Requirements

Citizens of the USA and Australia and holders of Hong Kong British passports need a visa from a local Japanese consulate if they wish to spend more than 72 hours in the country. New Zealanders may stay for up to 30 days without requiring a prior visa. Canadians, Scandinavians and Singaporeans may stay for 90 days without one, and Britons, the Irish, West Germans, Swiss and Austrians can arrive in the country without prior formalities and remain for up to 180 days.

There are no special health requirements unless the visitor comes from a country where there is cholera or yellow fever. (Anyone with a stiff leg or a bad back is advised to read the section about Japanese lavatories on page 123).

Customs

The following can be brought in duty free: three bottles of alcohol, 400 cigarettes (or 100 cigars, or 500 grams of tobacco), two ounces of perfume, two wrist watches and gifts up to a value of ¥100,000

Pornography is forbidden and the definition is a strict one.

Tourist Information Services, Tours and Guides

The Japan National Tourist Organization (JNTO) maintains offices abroad to disseminate information about travel in Japan. They have lists of travel companies offering inclusive tours to Japan and also detailed information about accommodation and transport. They sometimes have difficulty in answering specific questions about places and events. The following is a list of their overseas offices:

U.S.A.:	Rockefeller Plaza, 630 Fifth Ave.,	
	New York, N.Y. 10111.	TEL. (212) 757-5640.
	333 North Michigan Ave., Chicago, Ill. 60661	TEL. (312) 332-3975.
	1519 Main St., Suite 200, Dallas, Texas 75201.	TEL. (214) 741-4931.
	1737 Post St., San Francisco, Calif. 94115.	TEL. (415) 931-0700.

Kamakura Daibutsu (1252)

	624 South Grand Ave., Los Angeles, Calif. 90017.	TEL. (213) 623-1952.
	2270 Kalakaua Ave., Honolulu, Hawaii 96815.	TEL. (808) 923-7631.
Canada:	165 University Ave., Toronto, Ont. M5H 3B8.	TEL. (416) 366-7140.
England:	167 Regent St., London W. 1.	TEL. 734-9638.
Australia:	115 Pitt St., Sydney, N.S.W. 2000.	TEL. 232-4522.
Hong Kong:	Peter Bldg., 58 Queen's Road Central.	TEL: 5-227913.
Thailand:	56 Suriwong Road, Bangkok.	TEL. 233-5108.
France	4-8, rue Sainte-Anne, 75001 Paris.	TEL. 296-2029.
Switzerland:	Rue de Berne 13, Genève.	TEL. 318140.
Germany:	Biebergasse 6-10, 6000 Frankfurt a/M.	TEL. 20353.
Mexico:	Reforma 122, 5° Piso, B-2, México 6, D.F.	Tel. 535-85-83.
Brazil:	Av. Paulista, 509-S/405, 01311-Sào Paulo.	TEL. 289-2931.

Within Japan itself, JNTO have Tourist Information Centres (TIC) in Tokyo, Kyoto and in Narita Airport. The Tokyo branch, which is close to both the Hibiya and Ginza subway stations, is at 6-6, Yurakucho 1-chome, Chiyoda-ku, telephone (03) 502-1461. Pre-recorded information about the major events of the month in and around Tokyo can be obtained by ringing (03) 503-2911. The Kyoto branch is close to the railway station in the Kyoto Tower Building, Higashi-Shiokojicho, Shimogyo-ku, telephone (075) 371-5649. The Narita number is (0476) 32 8711.

Most of the real information in the TICs is under or behind the desk and can only be elicited by well-prepared questions. Leaflets in front of the centres are largely commercial in nature. The Tokyo TIC puts up a full list of events both in and outside the capital on its bulletin board.

In other cities the various tourist information offices serve domestic tourists and their staff rarely speak English. However there is an excellent free telephone scheme whereby any tourist, outside the city limits of Tokyo and Kyoto, can ring the aforementioned TICs for help, advice or information every day of the year between 9am and 5pm. This is done by simply depositing a ¥10 in a public telephone, dialling 106 and saying "Collect call, TIC". They even return the ¥10.

Local tours with English-speaking guides are operated by Japan Travel Bureau (JTB), Fujita Travel Service, Hankyu Express International, Hato Bus, Japan Gray Line, Tobu Travel Service and others. Lasting from a matter of hours to as long as a couple of weeks, these tours offer the visitor more flexibility than an all-inclusive tour from the visitor's home country. Accommodation, when provided, is usually in western-style hotels.

Professional guide-interpreters belonging to the Japan Guide Association can be hired through a Japanese travel agent. The basic daily fee is ¥12,000 to which other charges will be added. There are various schemes for foreigners to meet Japanese students learning English who will act as guides on an expenses-only basis. Arrangements can also be made to visit Japanese homes in the cities of Tokyo, Yokohama, Sapporo, Nagoya, Osaka, Kyoto, Otsu, Kobe, Kurashiki and Kagoshima. Information is available at the TICs.

Transport

International
By Air Most tourists arrive at the new Tokyo International Airport at Narita. This is 41 miles (66 km) and 1½ to 2 hours distance from the centre of the metropolis. Every visitor should consider the alternatives. Many airlines fly into the international airport at Osaka, an hour away from Kyoto. Nagoya and four airports on the island of Kyushu (Fukuoka, Nagasaki, Kumamoto and Kagoshima) have connections with South Korea

and Southeast Asia, notably Hong Kong. There are also designated international airports at Naha on Okinawa (for Southeast Asia), Komatsu near Kanazawa, Niigata (for Khabarovsk in the USSR) and Sapporo. Services are constantly changing and intending travellers should check all the details with a well-informed travel agent.

By Land and Sea There are only a few alternatives to arriving in an aeroplane. The best of these is to take the Trans-Siberian Railway from Europe across Siberia to Nakhodka, and from there by boat to Yokohama. There are also ferries from Pusan in South Korea to Shimonoseki, the western point of Honshu.

National

City To City By Air Narita is primarily an international airport: the domestic airport for Tokyo is at Haneda, much closer to the city centre. Nevertheless there are daily connections between Narita and some of the major cities, including Sapporo in Hokkaido and Fukuoka in Kyushu.

There are three main domestic airlines — JAL, ANA, TDA — flying to more than three dozen destinations throughout Japan, including a number of small and relatively inaccessible islands.

City To City By Train Japan has a comprehensive rail system and most foreign visitors use it in preference to other forms of transport. It is convenient and relatively simple to understand. Japanese passengers are invariably helpful to foreigners, making sure that they get off at the right places. Most lines are run by Japan Railways, the recently privatized group of seven companies that, has taken over the state run and loss making Japan National Railways. There are also other private railways that run efficient and economical services mainly in the kanto region. There are also other private railways, often cheaper and more efficient than JR, though obviously they are not in direct competition with the state railways.

The best known, JR service is the *Shinkansen*. Known as the 'Bullet Train' it travels at a speed of over 125 miles an hour (200 km an hour). There are three lines. The old one starts at Tokyo Station and travels past Mount Fuji to Nagoya, Kyoto, Osaka, Kobe, Himeji, Okayama, Miroshima and on to terminate at Fukuoka on the island of Kyushu. The whole journey takes less than seven hours. Two new lines opened in 1982. Both start from Omiya, just north of Tokyo. One goes across Honshu to Niigata on the Japan Sea opposite the island of Sado. The other *Shinkansen* line reaches north to Sendai and Morioka.

A special Japan Rail Pass is available that can be used on all JR transport, including the *Shinkansen*, ferryboats and buses. Valid for 7, 14 and 21 days respectively, there are two prices: green (or first class) and ordinary. They offer a good saving for restless, energetic travellers. The pass cannot be bought in Japan itself. An exchange order is purchased from an authorized travel agent (or from Japan Airlines) abroad and changed for the

Pachinko parlour, Osaka

pass itself on arrival in Japan.

City To City By Bus This is not much of an alternative to the train, but JNR do run a series of expressway buses from Tokyo to Nagoya, Kyoto and Osaka, including all night 'Dream' buses, which are popular with budget travellers.

Local Bus Lines Public bus systems radiate outwards from most railway stations. Foreign visitors who don't speak Japanese should get detailed instructions before venturing on one. Fares are generally charged according to distance and paid to the driver on leaving the bus.

Getting Around Within the Cities Tokyo, Yokohama, Nagoya, Osaka, Kyoto and Sapporo all have subways. This is both the simplest and the fastest means of travelling short distances. The underground systems are supplemented by overground train services, notably in central Tokyo with its excellent Yamanote and Chuo lines.

Subway network diagrams are published in English and station names are given using the Roman alphabet. In Tokyo the only major disadvantage of the subway is that it is often necessary to walk very considerable distances to change lines.

There are few streetcar lines left in Japan. The last in Tokyo, the Arakawa, covers an area few tourists ever see. Starting near Waseda University near Takadanobaba Station (Yamanote Line), it ends at Minowa near Minowa Sation (Hibiya Line).

200 mph Shinkansen 'Bullet Train'

The Kyoto trams are no more. To the great sorrow of all true lovers of the city they were removed at the end of the 1970s. Alas!

Taxis are more difficult to use than the subways. Drivers rarely speak English and Japanese cities are all subject to traffic jams, but the real problem is that Japanese addresses are peculiarly difficult to locate. Taxi drivers often hope to be guided by their passengers. When this is not possible, they drive round in circles consulting passersby and police boxes. They are rarely dishonest. Flagfall in Tokyo is ¥470 for the first two kilometres (1983).

Driving a Car This is the most satisfying way of seeing the real Japan, also the second most hazardous (after motorcycling, which is not covered in this book). The first problem is that there are no adequate large-scale maps with Latinized place names (*romaji*), nor will the driver find many *romaji* signs en route. Some skill has to be acquired in learning to recognize the Chinese characters, called *Kanji*, and Japanese syllable symbols, call *kana*, which indicate names.

The Japanese drive on the left, as in England. Expressway roads are excellent, but long stretches of mountain road can often be unsurfaced. Cities have complex one-way traffic systems, and in some of them the local drivers try to intimidate strangers. (Japanese number plates always give the district of registration of the car.) Japanese truck drivers are notoriously dangerous. However the biggest frustration — for Japanese and foreigners alike — is parking. In many cities, apart from hotels, the only available parking is provided by department stores, from which the driver is compelled to purchase goods, usually to the value of at least ¥1,000. Municipal carparks, where they exist, are very expensive.

Complex regulations make it impractical to buy a car in Japan and sell it a month or two later. It is possible to rent a car, or lease one, or indeed hire one with a driver. The price of petrol was around ¥165 a litre at the beginning of 1983.

The Japan Automobile Federation (JAF) offers to look after, on a reciprocal basis, members of the British, New Zealand, Hong Kong and Singapore AA, the American and Australian AAA, the Canadian CAA, the Dutch ANWB, the West German ADAC, and the Swiss TCI. Non-members of these organizations can join the JAF itself for ¥6,000. The federation publishes a booklet on driving in Japan (including all the traffic signs) called 'Rules of the Road' (¥1,000 plus postage). JAF is conveniently located right opposite Tokyo Tower at 3-5-8 Shiba-koen, Minato-ku, Tokyo 105, telephone (03) 436-2811.

Foreign drivers in Japan require an international driving licence.

International Communications

The International Telegraph and Telephone Office (KDD) handles all international telephone calls, telex, telegrams, photo-telegrams and facsimile telegrams in Japan.

International calls, via an English-speaking operator, can be obtained from any part of Japan by simply dialling 0051. Public phones can't be used but any commercial or private one (such as in a hotel or inn) will do. There is a three minute minimum charge for calls via the operator and these tend to be expensive. Collect calls (reverse charges) are usually cheaper.

Information on its other services can be obtained from the KDD information centres in Tokyo, telephone (03) 344 5151, and Osaka, telephone (06) 228 2300. They also have offices in Narita, Yokohama, Nagoya, Kyoto, Kobe, Hiroshima, Fukuoka and Okinawa.

The Japanese post office offers a reliable service.

English-language Media

For a nation of self-confessed 'poor English speakers' the Japanese have surprisingly good English-language media. Each of the major Japanese newspapers publishes a slim English edition. *The Daily Yomiuri* and *The Mainichi Daily News* appear in the morning, and the *Asahi Evening News* comes out in the afternoon. Many foreign residents nevertheless prefer the independent newspaper called *The Japan Times*. Unfortunately these publications are difficult to get outside the half dozen largest cities.

Tokyo Journal offers the best coverage of events in the capital and has interesting articles about Japanese life and culture. It is essential reading for any visitor staying for more than a few days. *Kansai Time Out* has very comprehensive coverage of the Kyoto, Osaka, Kobe area and can be similarly recommended. *The Monthly Hokkaido* has information about Japan's northern island. These publications are normally available at the tourist information centres.

Most inns and hotels provide television. Sets with the multiplex facility offer a choice of Japanese or foreign language sound for some programmes originally made abroad, particularly films. Cable television with programmes in English is available in large hotels in Tokyo, Kyoto, Osaka and Kobe. The one English language radio station is called FEN (for Far East Network).

Money

The currency of Japan is the *yen*, which is pronounced *en*. It is not subdivided. Foolhardy guidebooks give an exchange rate to the US dollar. It should be sufficient to note here that the yen rate had dropped to under 150 to the dollar by 1987. From time to time there have been rumours that a 'new yen' would be issued at 100 or 1,000 times the value of the present one. So far this hasn't happened.

There are relatively fewer banks in Japan willing to change traveller's cheques than almost anywhere else in Asia. Only specially designated branches can change traveller's cheques, or indeed foreign currency. Large hotels can *sometimes* change money, and are *sometimes* willing to do so for non-residents.

Credit cards are also difficult to use, except in sophisticated western restaurants and hotels. They are rarely useful in any Japanese-style establishment. The Japanese prefer cash.

The only practical alternative to carrying a lot of money around is to open a post office savings account. This can be accomplished without formalities and only a small deposit, but all transactions have to be written in Japanese, so special assistance is required by the foreign user. The post office will also ask for a Japanese address.

There is no tipping in Japan, and foreign visitors should not try to introduce the custom as it will cause embarrassment.

Shopping

Department Stores Japan is a paradise for people who enjoy department stores. The great Japanese retailers have a baroque splendour. In Kyoto Daimaru for example, the day begins with a stately Mozart dance. Senior managers greet the first customers with bows at the entrance, while the staff stand erect and motionless at their counters — but only for a couple of minutes — then the store is transformed into a seething mass of nervous commercial activity.

Specialist pickle shop, Kyoto

Morning market, Takayama

Each store has six to ten separate floors and stocks an extraordinarily comprehensive range of goods. Visitors can usually obtain an English-language store guide (or directory) from the information desk (always indicated in English) on the first floor (i.e. ground floor).

About half the area of an average store is used to sell clothes, including the traditional Japanese dress called *kimono*. All the stores have a range of articles for use in the home and garden, some have exhibition halls and art galleries. Most have extensive food shops, and many foreign visitors may consider buying cooked foods there, rather than paying for meals in hotels, inns or restaurants. Department stores often contain half a dozen or more of their own coffee shops and restaurants, some of which may be open in the evening. All in all, the large department store is an authentic microcosm of Japan itself — and there is no Japanese city without one.

In Tokyo the big stores are at Nihombashi, Ginza and major railway stations. Until recently the grand old establishments of Nihombashi, Mitsukoshi (with Trafalgar Square replicated lions) and Takashimaya ('of the rose') had the biggest sales. However the enormous Seibu built above Ikebukuro Station, owned by a private railway, with a total floor area of 17.8 acres (72,000 square metres) is arguably the world's largest shop.

Photographic Equipment Japan's main discount camera shops are at Tokyo's Shinjuku Station. The best known names are Yodobashi, Doi,

Victoria, and Sakuraya. The shops all have duty free departments for foreign customers. Serious shoppers should check prices and bargain before buying. Japanese-made equipment *can* be as cheap as in Hong Kong if the visitor buys shrewdly. The Shinjuku shops also offer the lowest prices for film of any place in Japan.

The main drawback to shopping at these stores is that they are intolerably noisy: many retailers in Japan believe that loud music, public announcements and shouting increase sales, presumably by weakening the psychological resistance of customers.

Audio Equipment A wide range of electrical appliances and electronic equipment is sold around Akihabara Station in Tokyo. The prices are the lowest in Japan and competition between the shops is intense. Some of the stores have large branches devoted to duty-free selling. The atmosphere of Akihabara is more like the central areas of Hong Kong than anywhere else in Japan.

Anyone buying equipment should be aware of the differences between Japan and other countries in terms of voltages and other matters. Some appliances may only work in Japan, some may only work abroad, others are convertible. The voltage in Japan is 100, 50 cycles in eastern Japan, 60 cycles in western Japan. The FM radio frequencies are between 80 and 90 mHz.

Bookshops In Tokyo the leading bookshops selling English-language publications are Maruzen (opposite the Takashimaya Department Store in Nihombashi), Kinokuniya (on the east side of Shinjuku) and Jena (in Ginza). All have a comprehensive selection of books on Japan, international newspapers and magazines, and general literature. Major hotels have small bookshops. There are many second-hand bookstores in the Kanda Jimbocho area of Tokyo, around the Sanseido bookshop. Some sell old Japanese *ukiyo-e* prints.

Antiques The Japanese may not be as interested in old artifacts as Europeans, but there are antique shops scattered throughout the country. In Tokyo there are half a dozen antique markets held on special days of the month outside shrines and temples. Detailed information is published in the *Tokyo Antiques News*, available at the Tourist Information Centres. The Tokyo Old Folkcraft and Antiques Hall is open daily at 23-1 Kanda Jimbocho 1-chome, Chiyoda-ku, telephone (03) 295 7112. It has a fine mixture of quality and junk and is just behind the aforementioned Sanseido bookshop.

Crafts Ceramics, lacquer, textiles, metalwork, hand-made paper, wooden and bamboo articles and other traditional craft products are on sale in department stores and speciality shops throughout Japan, but the official promotional organization is at the Japan Traditional Craft Centre at Plaza 246, 1-1 Minami Aoyama 3-chome, Minato-ku, Tokyo 107, telephone (03) 403 2460. The centre has a small permanent exhibition (all the articles are for sale), special displays put on by the different craft industries, and a great deal of information on regional centres and craft techniques. There is an extensive video library, freely accessible to visitors. The centre should be able to answer any specific enquiries.

A Japanese bamboo basket may cost a hundred times more than one in China. Japanese crafts are the fruit of a collective imagination and a great artistic tradition. Finishing is superlative. Craftsmen are honoured members of society and their products are valued accordingly.

Outdoor Sport and Recreation

Four-fifths of Japan's land area is mountainous. The landscape has been created around a series of chains of volcanic mountains, many of them still active, in which there are almost 2,000 major hot springs. Areas of outstanding natural beauty are protected by national and quasi-national parks. There are 74 of them in all, occupying over eight percent of the land.

No less beautiful than Asia's other great archipelagos, Indonesia and the Philippines, Japan has well-developed facilities for visitors who want to spend time in the open air. Foreigners should not find the mountains lonely. Many visitors will make more friends in the countryside (with young Japanese on holiday) than in the big cities.

Several national parks are famous for their magnificent alpine flora in late summer. These include the Hakusan and Chubu Sangaku national parks of central Honshu, Nikko north of Tokyo, the Towada Hachimantai National Park in northeastern Honshu, and the Daisetsuzan in Hokkaido. Late summer coincides with the official climbing seasons for most of the mountains, when they are considered 'safe'. Mount Fuji for example, Japan's highest mountain (12,388 feet, or 3,776 metres) which has many different kinds of vegetation, is open to climbers from July 1st to August 31st. Regrettably there is still no guide in English to the wild flowers of the Japanese countryside.

Mount Fuji is an easy climb, taking five or six hours only. In fact the Japanese tend to describe both mountaineering and simply walking in the mountains as 'mountain climbing'. Some of the ascents in the Japan Alps, Yari-ga-take (10,433 feet, 3,180 metres) for example, are very difficult, but many of the popular peaks can be climbed in a matter of a few hours up well marked trails. Good maps of the mountains, as well as the national parks, are published but the legends are in Japanese, so that some prior explanation of them is necessary. The Japan Mountaineering Association is at the Kishi Memorial Gymnasium, 1-1 Jinnan 1-chome, Shibuya-ku, Tokyo, telephone (03) 460 2006. Orienteering is also popular in Japan and the national organization is the Japan Orienteering Committee at Mori Building Number 34, 25-5 Toranomon 1-chome, Minato-ku, Tokyo.

(Preceding page) Cherry blossom (sakura) festival, Ueno Park, Tokyo

Each winter more than ten million young Japanese ski. The resorts close to the Tokyo conurbation, particularly those in Nagano and Niigata Prefectures, are crowded; those in northeastern Honshu and Hokkaido are rather less so. Many of the ski resorts are also spas, so skiers can relax in communal hot spring baths after a day's skiing. This is a luxury enjoyed outside Japan probably by only the Californians. Skiing is big business and the visitor will find no problem in getting information. The Ski Association of Japan is at the Kishi Memorial Gymnasium (the same address as the Mountaineering Association, above).

Throughout the countryside there is abundant wildlife. There are still brown bears in Hokkaido and some black bears in Honshu, also wild boar and Kamoshika antelope. These are rarely seen, unlike the indigenous Japanese monkeys, which have learnt to stop motorists for food and take baths in hot springs. At the other end of the ecological scale insect life is abundant. No visitor coming in the summer will forget the butterflies, dragonflies, and cicadas.

Japan is of special interest to ornithologists. Any birdwatchers considering a trip will discover comprehensive information available in English (more so than for any other outdoor activity). This is due to the impressive Wild Bird Society of Japan, which has 64 chapters throughout Japan. In 1982 the society published *A Field Guide to the Birds of Japan* with colour illustrations of all of Japan's 537 species of birds (following the Peterson system), together with information about birdwatching locales. The book costs ¥ 2,900 and is available from the society at its address: Aoyama Flower Building, 1-4 Shibuya 1-chome, Shibuya-ku, Tokyo 150. Their telephone number is (03) 406 7141.

Angling, both freshwater and sea, is popular. For some reason foreigners are said to have found the sport unsatisfactory in Japan. A matter of tackle? The national body is the Japan Angling Association at the JAC Building, 31-4 Yushima 3-chome, Bunkyo-ku, Tokyo, telephone (03) 833 6787.

A small but growing number of foreigners are cycling in Japan. It is possible to obtain collapsible touring bikes that can be taken on trains. There is also an organization of cheap cycling inns, which hire out bicycles. The Japan Cycling Association is at Jitensha Kaikan Number 3 Building, 9-3 Akasaka 1-chome, Minato-ku, Tokyo, telephone number (03) 583 5628.

The best place to buy sports equipment is the Kanda Jimbocho area of Tokyo, particularly in and around the Mizuno Corporation of 22 Kanda Ogawa-cho 3-chome, Chiyoda-ku, Tokyo, telephone (03) 294 1211. However equipment is not particularly cheap in Japan and large sizes may not be available. The shops also carry little stock of items they consider unseasonal.

(It should be noted that communication with all Japanese organizations, such as the ones listed above, is problematic. Much depends on the person answering the enquiry. In general asking in person is preferable to speaking on the phone. If communication is still difficult, visitors should ask staff at the Tourist Information Centres to interpret.)

The Arts, Entertainment and Nightlife

The Polite Arts The Japanese enjoy a respite from the pressures of their modern world by practising certain traditional arts. Most of these are well known abroad. There is the tea ceremony or *chanoyu*, the art of flower arranging called *ikebana*, and the cultivation of miniature trees or *bonsai*, in addition to *origami* or paperfolding, calligraphy, painting and playing solo musical instruments such as the *koto*, a form of harp.

Foreign visitors intent on a rapid absorption of Japanese culture can see the tea ceremony and flower arrangement, and hear *koto* (together with other programmes) in less than an hour at Gion Corner, the Gion Kaburenjo Theatre, Gion Machi Minamigawa, Kyoto, telephone (075) 561 1115. The performance is twice daily between March and November. There is nothing quite as ambitious in Tokyo, although JTB Sunrise Tours have a weekly 'Art-Around-Town' charabanc.

A real appreciation of these arts depends on some knowledge of their basic philosophy, and a good deal of concentration, if not meditation. The tea ceremony in particular is not a spectator sport, but an expression of some of the most important values of the Japanese. The two principal schools, Ura Senke and Omote Senke, are both based in Kyoto, in fact next to each other: Ogawa-dori Teranouchi, Kamigyo-ku, Kyoto, telephone (075) 431 3111 (Ura Senke) and (075) 432 1111 (Omote Senke). Information about flower arranging is available from Ikebana International, which represents all the major schools, at the Shufunotomo Building, 6 Kanda Surugadai 1-chome, Chiyoda-ku, Tokyo, telephone (03) 293 8188.

Visual Arts Japanese art and archaeology is best represented at the Tokyo National Museum, 1 Ueno Park, Taito-ku, Tokyo, telephone (03) 822 1111, but the country has more than 350 other major museums and galleries displaying Japanese, Korean, Chinese and western art. In addition there are the commercial art galleries, department store museums and galleries, and photography galleries.

Many of the larger institutions show their collections in rotation. Temple treasure houses are often only open at special times. The best time for seeing the fullest displays of national treasures is the second half of October and November.

The essential reference book for anyone considering a visit for the purpose of seeing Japanese art is *Roberts' Guide to Japanese Museums* by L P Roberts (Kodansha International Limited, Tokyo, New York and San Francisco, 1978).

Kabuki theatre, Ginza

The classics of Japanese cinema are best seen outside Japan. The masters of the 1930s, 1940s and 1950s are more highly regarded in New York and London than in Tokyo, and the films that are shown abroad have English-language subtitles. The National Film Centre comes under the National Museum of Modern Art and is located at 7-6 Kyobashi 3-chome, Chuo-ku, Tokyo, telephone (03) 561 0823. It shows classic Japanese and foreign films for the nominal price of ¥250 a seat. There are many commerical cinemas.

Dramatic Arts *Kabuki* is the spectacular, stylized form of theatre popular in the cities for over 300 years. It is regularly performed at the Kabukiza, National Theatre, and Shimbashi Embujo in Tokyo, the Minamiza in Kyoto and the Shin Kabukiza in Osaka. The Kabukiza, in particular, goes out of its way to help foreign visitors. It offers English-language printed programmes, earphone commentary in English and even a 10 percent discount for foreigners. *The Kabuki Handbook* by a S and G M Halford (Charles E Tuttle Company, Rutland and Tokyo, 1956) is invaluable.

Bunraku is the puppet theatre of Osaka. It can best be seen at the Asahiza in Osaka's Dotombori entertainment district.

No (also sometimes spelt *noh*) dates back to the 14th century, and is a theatrical form combining drama, poetry, music, and dance. It is very slow and while this in itself is mesmerizing, the *no* can only be appreciated by the foreigner who takes along a translation. Poetry is the dominant

Sumo wrestling, Kokugikan Stadium, Tokyo

element in the form. While there are many *no* theatres throughout the country regular performances are held only in Tokyo and Kyoto: in Tokyo visitors may try the Kanze Kaikan, 16-4 Shoto 1-chome, Shibuya-ku, telephone (03) 469 5241.

Martial Arts *Aikido*, *judo*, and *karate* are all forms of unarmed combat, while *kendo* is the Japanese style of fencing. The World Headquarters for aikido is at 102 Wakamatsu-cho, Shinjuku-ku, Tokyo, telephone (03) 203 9236. Judo is taught at the Kodokan, 16-30 Kasuga 1-chome, Bunkyo-ku, Tokyo, telephone (03) 811 7151. The Japan Karate Association international headquarters is at 6-1 Ebisu Nishi 1-chome, Shibuya-ku, Tokyo, telephone (03) 462 1415. The All Japan Kendo Federation is at the Budokan, 2 Kitanomaru Koen, Chiyoda-ku, Tokyo, telephone (03) 211 5804.

Sumo wrestling is the national sport. Originating in Japan perhaps as early as AD 200, professional 15-day tournaments are now great spectacles with many fans among the foreign residents of Japan. Three tournaments are held each year in Tokyo, in January, May and September. Osaka has a tournament in March, while Nagoya has one in July, and Fukuoka (Kyushu) in November. The most important fights are in the late afternoon, and are televised. Buying tickets is not always easy, particularly for the final weekend of a tournament. Reserving tickets from abroad is probably impossible. Tokyo tournament tickets are best obtained from the hall: Kokugikan, 1-9 Kuramae 2-chome, Taito-ku, Tokyo, telephone (03) 623 5111.

Music The Japanese have a voracious appetite for every kind of musical experience. *Gagaku* is the ancient court orchestral music, sometimes performed at shrines and temples. *Minyo* is folksong, best heard during local festivals. *Enka* is the folksy, maudlin indigenous popular song.

Western classical music is performed with brilliance: Tokyo alone has six symphony orchestras. Jazz has a great following. Westernized pop includes rock, new wave, 'new music' (lyrical rock), and a lot of sugary, bouncy songs for younger teenagers. (See also Nightlife below.)

Nightlife *Mizu shobai*, 'water business' (euphemistic for alcohol business), is one of Japan's largest, most profitable and most diversified industries. If the Japanese cultivate respectability, they are also among the world's most serious hedonists. There is little hypocrisy and less prudery. The basic attractions are food and drink (see Eating and Drinking on page 130), music and dancing, the (professional) company of women or (more rarely) that of men — and sex. No city in Japan can really compare with Tokyo but the liveliest places outside the capital are Osaka and Sapporo. In Tokyo every Japanese whim has its price, and most western ones can be satisfied as well. Nevertheless the night world is the most difficult one for the foreigner to find his or her way in; Japanese friends make invaluable companions.

The traditionalist male-oriented nightlife of geisha parties and hostess bars, typically in Tokyo's Akasaka and Ginza areas, is extremely expensive and likely to be boring for those who don't speak Japanese. Even for local people the final bill is an unpredictable event, more worrying for those without an expense account than for those who do have one. Akasaka and Ginza also have large old-fashioned night clubs with floor shows. Cover charges are around ¥6,000 per person, on top of which there are fees for hostesses and drink charges.

Tokyo has some splendid live music clubs, where foreigners will feel very welcome. They are generally inexpensive with cover charges of ¥2,000 to 5,000 a head. Many play jazz but there are also rock, country and western, new wave, 'new music', and samba clubs. The best known jazz house is the Roppongi Pit Inn, 17-4 Roppongi 3-chome, Minato-ku, Tokyo, telephone (03) 585 1063.

In Tokyo there are discos in Harajuku, Shibuya, and Shinjuku but the greatest concentration is at Roppongi. This is the playground *par excellence* of the foreign community. For the Japanese Roppongi represents the most westernized corner of their country. There are few hostesses and the sexes are only unequal to the extent that men have to pay more for admissions than women. Roppongi has been described as 'pick-up Tokyo'. Visitors will inevitably gravitate towards a tall building with flashing lights called Roppongi Square, which houses a different disco on every floor: 5 Roppongi 3-chome, Minato-ku, Tokyo. Charges are in the same range as those for live music clubs.

By American standards Japanese cities are very safe and well policed. Subway trains finish early, around midnight in Tokyo, in an apparently futile attempt by the authorities to moderate the consumption of alcohol, but there are plenty of taxis.

(*Tokyo Journal*, a monthly publication, lists events, concerts, theatres, restaurants, live music clubs and discos in the capital. And it has maps with the locations of the places listed.)

Festivals

Japan still maintains many of the traditions of a pre-industrial society. If some customs have inevitably been lost, others have been enhanced in scope and increased in popularity. A hundred years or so ago some folk traditions were regarded as 'primitive' and so discontinued. Today towns throughout the country publicize their local festivals to attract visitors from other parts of the country — and not all the events are traditional.

Matsuri, which are usually translated by the English word 'festivals', cover a wide range of occasions from purely private family gatherings to mass celebrations throughout the length and breadth of cities. Originally all religious, many are now secular. Some are quiet, sober, well-ordered, static affairs; others are noisy, bacchanalian, dynamic, even anarchic. Matsuri encompass street festivals, pageants, masquerades, carnivals, tournaments, races, and Shinto and Buddhist ceremonies. Many of them are processions.

The Japanese festival is primarily a communal celebration — an affirmation of roots. Nevertheless foreign visitors will rarely feel excluded from this experience. It is far commoner for the foreigner to end up right in the centre of things, dancing, playing drums or whatever — and not lacking for *sake*. Even the most blatantly commercial of the festivals (and there are some) have a kind of electric excitement that is especially Japanese, but the visitor should be under no illusion that the biggest festivals are the best. Some of the most interesting festivals take place each year in obscure villages with no tourists and no photographers.

There are eight nation wide festivals. The New Year is celebrated on the first three days of January, followed by Setsubun, the beginning of spring, in early February. March 3rd is the Girls' Festival; the Festival of the Buddha's Birthday is on April 8th; the Boys' Festival is May 5th. Tanabata, the 7th night of the 7th month, is a festival held on July 7th to honour two lovers who became the stars Vega and Altair, only permitted to meet on this one night of the year. Obon in mid-July is a joyful festival when the dead return from the spirit world to rejoin their families for three days. Shichigosan on November 15th is a celebration for children who have attained the ages of three, five or seven.

In most parts of Japan the national festivals tend to be quiet family celebrations. The liveliest are Tanabata and Obon. However it should be

シェーキーズ
ピザパーラー
SHAKEY'S
ピザと
映画と
音楽と
PIZZA PARLOR
SHAKEY'S
GALLERY
TAMAYA
アネックス
メガネ
TAMAYA
らん月
しゃぶしゃぶ
Sukiyaki
BEEF
STEAK
らん月
ステーキコーナー
B1F
テーラー
ロンフォード
5F
高梨歯科
☎(567)3718
4F
サエグサ画廊
B1~3F
プロポーションアカデミー
国武株式会社
デイリークイーン
ニコン
Nikon
Salon
サロン
MATSUSHIMA
井上商会
ローンス
インド
ハクビ京都きもの学院
紀伊産業
ミハラヤ
music records & tapes
十字屋
大和銀行
中央美術画廊
ようこそ
銀座へ

noted that whereas Japan now uses the Gregorian calendar (albeit with imperial reign years), these festivals, together with the New Year, are celebrated in many places according to the old lunar calendar, about a month later than the dates given above.

Local festivals can be more enjoyable than the national ones. Many of them take place in the months of April, May, June and August. There are quite a number in June and October, fewer at other times of the year. There is no city, probably no town without its festival.

The best available information about local events is probably that provided by the Tourist Information Centres in Japan (see page 20). Japan National Tourist Organization offices abroad have little information, though hopefully this may change. Information provided by guidebooks is sporadic at best. JTB tours, starting in Tokyo, cover 14 of the major festivals between February 1st and November 3rd each year. Of these their tour to the three big festivals of Tohoku in early August is possibly the most exciting.

DESTINATIONS

The Tokyo Region (Kanto)

Kanto, sometimes called the National Capital Region, is the eastern central part of Honshu, the main island of Japan. Facing the Pacific Ocean to the south and east, surrounded by mountains to the north and west, the heart of the region is the great Kanto Plain. This is the largest area of flat, cultivable land in the country, though much of it has now been swallowed up by urban and industrial development. It is the most industrialized of the eight regions into which Japan is officially divided: nearly 30 percent of the whole Japanese population lives on the Kanto Plain.Japan; it is the

Kanto is rivalled in historical importance only by the region of Kyoto, Nara and Osaka. Kanto rose to prominence after the central western part of Honshu but by the 12th century it was sufficiently developed to become the military and political base of the ruler of Japan, Minamoto Yoritomo. His headquarters was at Kamakura, where the government of the shogunate remained until the 14th century. Kanto was again the home of the shogunate, or military dictatorship, from the 17th to the 19th centuries, when the Tokugawa family established themselves in Edo, to be renamed Tokyo in 1868 when it replaced Kyoto as the formal capital of Japan and the residence of the Emperor.

If much of the centre of Kanto is Japanese-style urban sprawl, there is fine country to be visited on the fringes of the plain. The Nikko National

THE TOKYO REGION (KANTO)

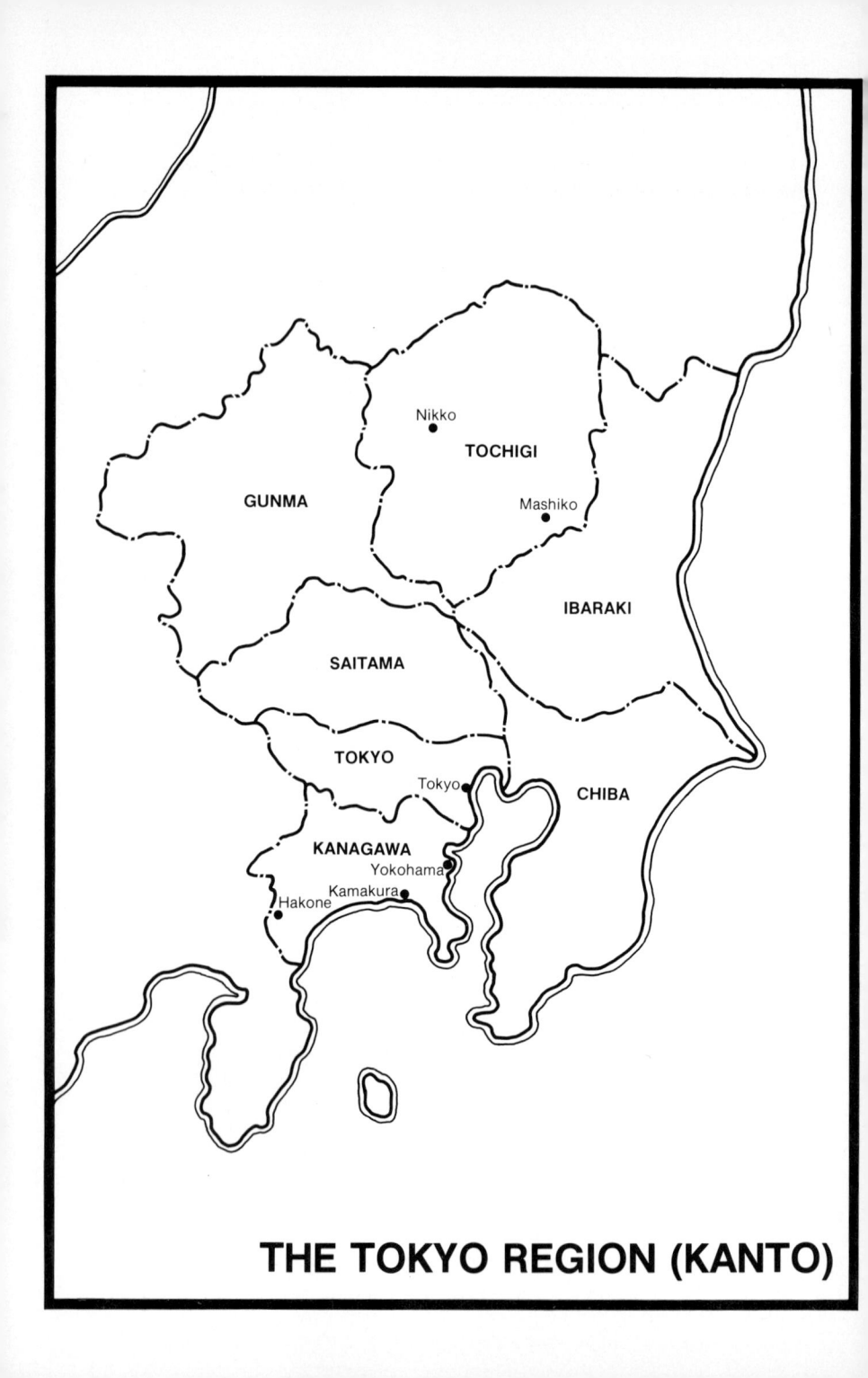

Park, in Tochigi Prefecture in the north, has volcanic landscapes in addition to the mausoleum of the founder of the Tokugawa Shogunate. There are splendid sheer mountains in the Joshin-etsu Kogen National Park on the northern border of Gunma Prefecture, and there are also the Chichibu-Tama National Park and the Fuji-Hakone-Izu National Park, both within easy striking distance of Tokyo.

Tokyo

It is an understatement to refer to Tokyo as the capital of Japan; it is the ultimate megapolis of the 20th century. Twenty-five and a half million hyper-active, hyper-intelligent citizens have combined their resources to put on the ultimate human happening, the ultimate human spectacle. For the foreign visitor it seems more of a jungle than darkest Zaire. It is a city of illuminated signs, signals, signposts, and maps (lots of maps pointing every direction except north), few of which the visitor can read, almost none of which the visitor can understand. It is not a destination neatly packaged with sightseeing attractions, unlike many other Japanese cities and towns. This city of excitatory phenomena requires the traveller to become a kind of urban explorer, promised unique, personal experiences and the unfailing courtesy, support and friendship of the most generous of big city people.

Sizing Up the Tokyo Conurbation

Tokyo is the largest city in the world, though not always recognized as such. In official statistics the population is sometimes given as eight million, sometimes 11.4 million. The former is for the residents of the inner city (the 23 special wards), the latter figure is for the Tokyo Metropolis, a curious entity that combines the inner city, the western suburbs and some countryside beyond it (including a mountain 6,620 feet or 2,018 metres high), the seven islands of Izu south of Tokyo Bay, and the Ogasawara Islands far to the south, ranging no less than 600 to 800 miles (1,000 to 1,300 km) from the centre of the metropolis.

Forgetting about scenic mountains and semi-tropical islands, but including all the dormitory cities and industrial centres which are fully integrated into the economy of Tokyo, the extent of the southern Kanto urban sprawl, the population rises to about 26.3 million. This is the best figure. Mexico City, sometimes claimed as the biggest in the world, has a conurbation figure of only 14.5 million, though the city figure is over 9 million (1979). The New York conurbation is larger, over 16 million, but the city is smaller, 7 million (1980). Shanghai has 11 million citizens, but of these 5 million are peasants working on communes surrounding the city. Beijing may be a contender one day, but the North China conurbation at present is not more than about 16 million strong.

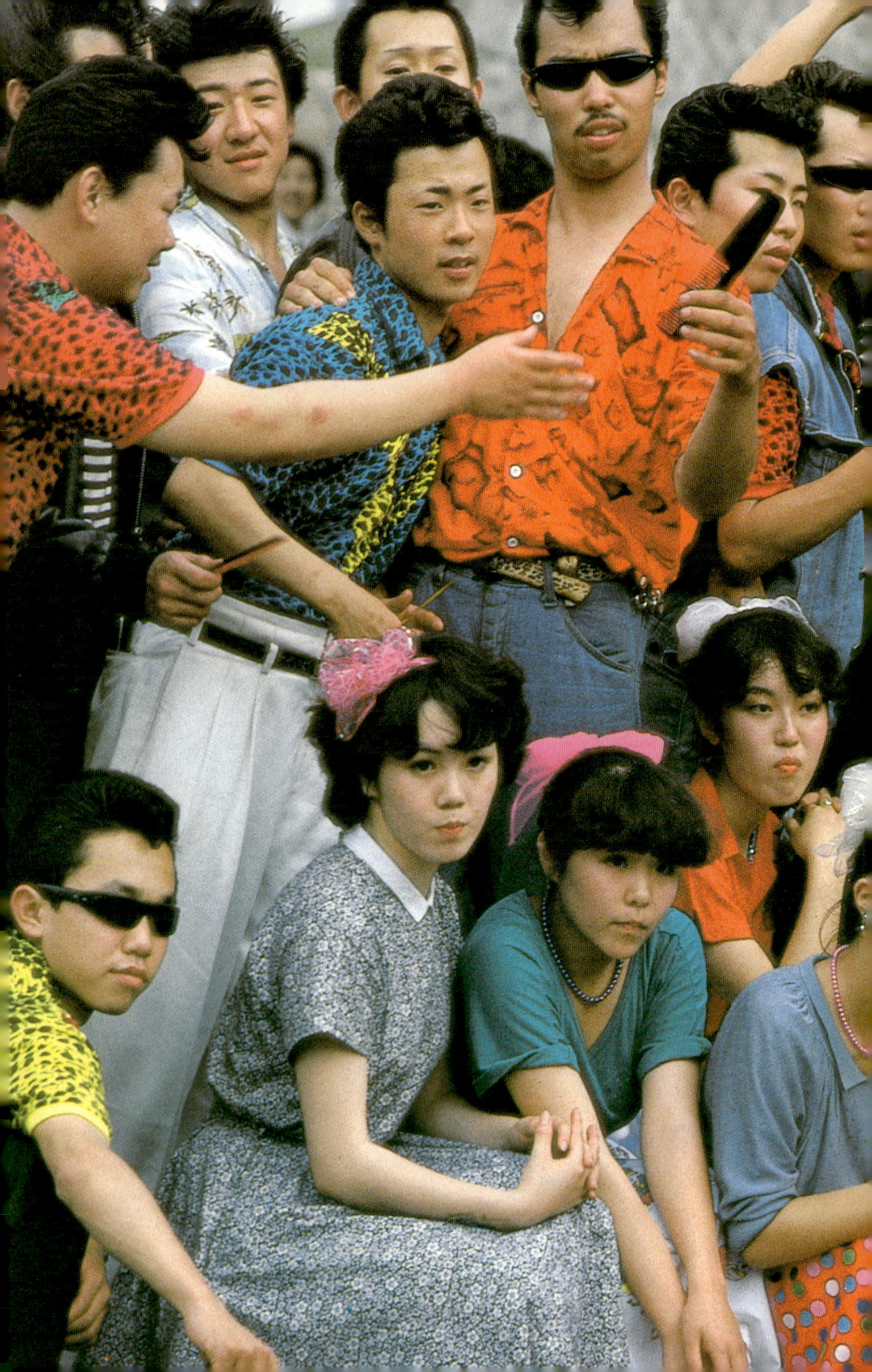

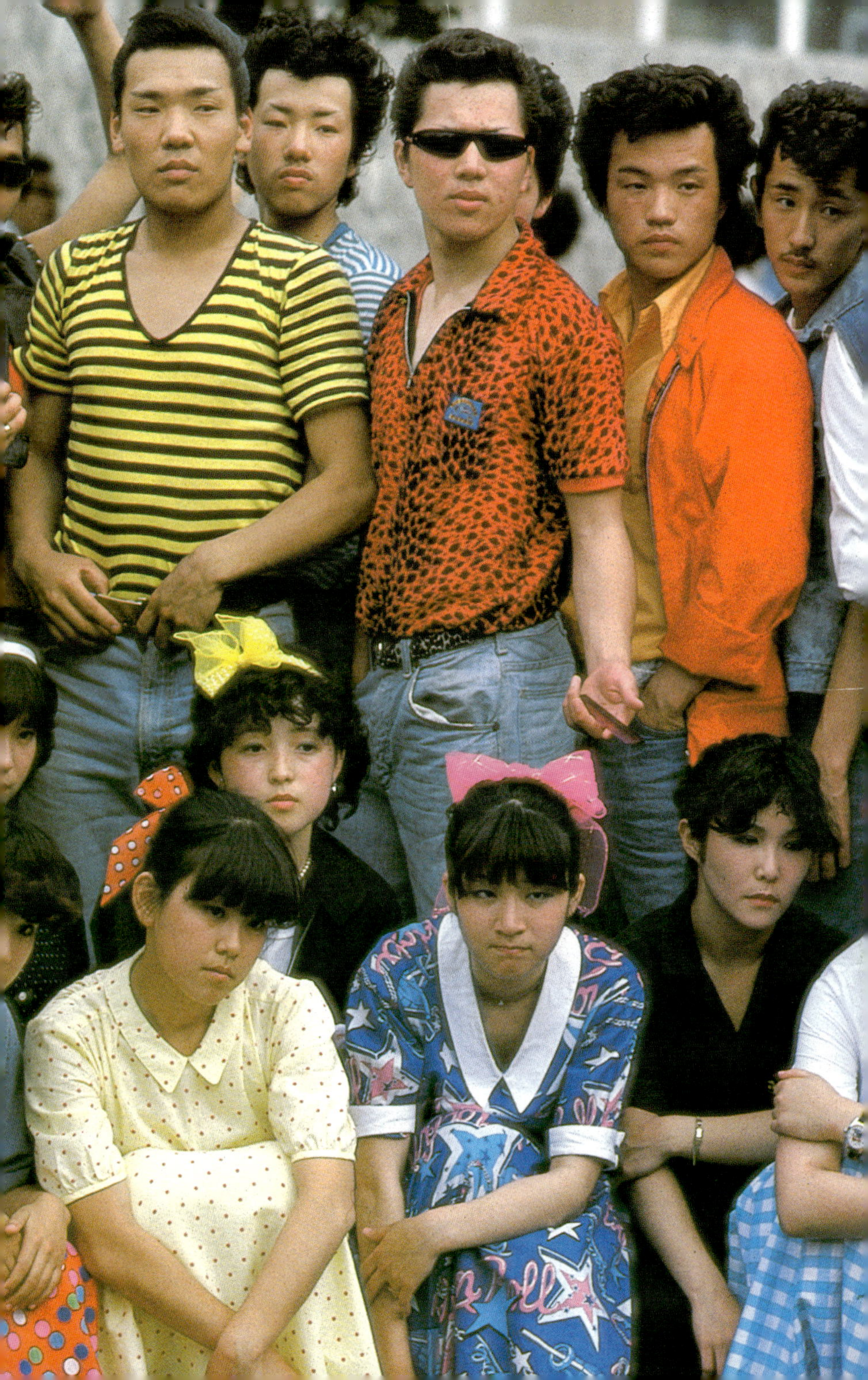

(Preceding page) 'Takenoku Yoku', (50's fashion revival) Harajiku, Tokyo

The Real Tokyo Life-style

Foreigners sometimes assume that because districts like Marunouchi and Ginza have streets like those in London or New York, Tokyo is therefore a western as opposed to a 'Japanese' city. This is a misconception. Residential Tokyo is still something quite different from anything in the west, just as the basic style of life is entirely different.

In many areas the population density is as high as 40,000 people per square mile (15,000 per square km), but half the inhabitants, even of the central districts, still live in one or two storey wooden buildings. Only 10 percent of the houses have more than 1,075 square feet (100 square metres) floor space. The houses tend to be close together: 30 percent have no direct sunlight. Many are without baths: the public bath house usually serves as the social centre of the neighbourhood. Access to the buildings is often only through narrow alleys, difficult to reach in the case of fire. Tokyo still has the worst record in the country in this respect: 8,000 fires in 1978 in which 142 people died. In many areas nightwatchmen still patrol, banging wooden blocks, the signal for vigilance against fires.

If housing is poor by western standards, the Japanese spend comparatively little time at home, and little money on their houses, only 10 percent of household incomes to be precise. Tokyo people have large disposable incomes to devote to satisfying their restless energies. They spend more money on food, clothing, and entertainment (in that order) than on housing. The cash goes on eating and drinking out, going to films, discos, live music shows, concerts, galleries, museums, festivals, sport and a hundred other leisure activities aided and abetted by the temptations offered by the amazing, labyrinthine department stores. Tokyo is an exciting place.

The metropolis also seems crazy, sometimes almost comic to the foreign visitor. Tokyo is the only major city in the world trying to be sophisticated in two cultures rather than one, and sometimes it doesn't succeed. There is no city where English (not to mention French and German) is so widely used with so little sense. The frenetic hedonism of the place appears almost serious to the relaxed westerner. The people of Tokyo, not least the late-night drunks, live for the day, live for the hour, with a determination which can probably only be explained in the context of the tragic history of the city, which everybody would prefer to forget.

History

As early as the 12th century there was a settlement called Edo (Estuary) but it was insignificant until a lord called Ota Dokan (1432-1486) built a castle there in 1457. Ota was assassinated and Edo declined until Tokugawa Ieyasu (1542-1616) rebuilt the castle in 1590, after receiving the fiefdom from the all-powerful Hideyoshi. When the latter died in 1598 Ieyasu seized power, becoming shogun in 1603.

The Tokugawa remained in Edo and the city prospered. Not only was the city the location of the administration of the shogunate, but the feudal lords were also required to maintain households in Edo. This was part of a highly successful system to prevent revolts: the lords tended to dissipate their savings and the Tokugawa leaders were able to seize hostages at will. The Edo merchants, in particular, benefited. There was a great development of bourgeois culture (including for example the kabuki and *ukiyo-e* woodblock printing). By the beginning of the 18th century the city had over one million inhabitants, possibly the largest city in the world at that time.

Unfortunately Edo was the antithesis of a well-planned city. It was laid out as a Japanese feudal castle town, in other words like a maze. Unlike Kyoto with its regular Chinese grid pattern the layout of Edo was completely irregular, designed to mislead an invading army rather than promote maximum ease of communications. One result of this strange form of urban development was that Edo suffered from repeated fires. Two-thirds of the city was destroyed in 1657 and more than 100,000 people died. Edo was rebuilt just as before and more fires followed. They were called 'the flowers of Edo'.

In 1868 Edo was renamed Tokyo (Eastern Palace) and the castle became the Imperial Palace. The last Tokugawa shogun gave up his office and the Emperor came to live in the new imperial capital. This was the beginning of the Meiji era which lasted until 1912, a time when the inhabitants of the capital were increasingly influenced by the European and American way of life.

Throughout the Meiji era and afterwards the city kept on growing. The population was 1.8 million in 1919 and it had reached 2.3 million when disaster again struck Tokyo. In 1923 an earthquake occurred followed by fires that left 100,000 dead, 1.5 million homeless, and 40 percent of the city destroyed.

Tokyo was rebuilt in the midst of a construction boom, expanded once more and the city boundaries were enlarged. Some wide streets were built to allow modern transportation systems to be introduced. Achieving 6.6 million by 1944, the city was again destroyed, this time more comprehensively than ever before. Towards the close of the Second World War, American forces launched no less than 102 bombing raids against the Japanese capital. The worst was on March 10th, 1945 when 130 B-29s dropped incendiary bombs in parallel lines across the city. Officially about 168,000 people died, and 80 percent of the buildings of the capital were destroyed.

After the war Tokyo once again rose from its ashes. Sheltering only 2.8 million people in 1945, there were 4.2 million two years later. Within the borders of the Tokyo Metropolis the population grew rapidly to reach a peak in 1965, when the figure was 8.9 million. This was also the worst year

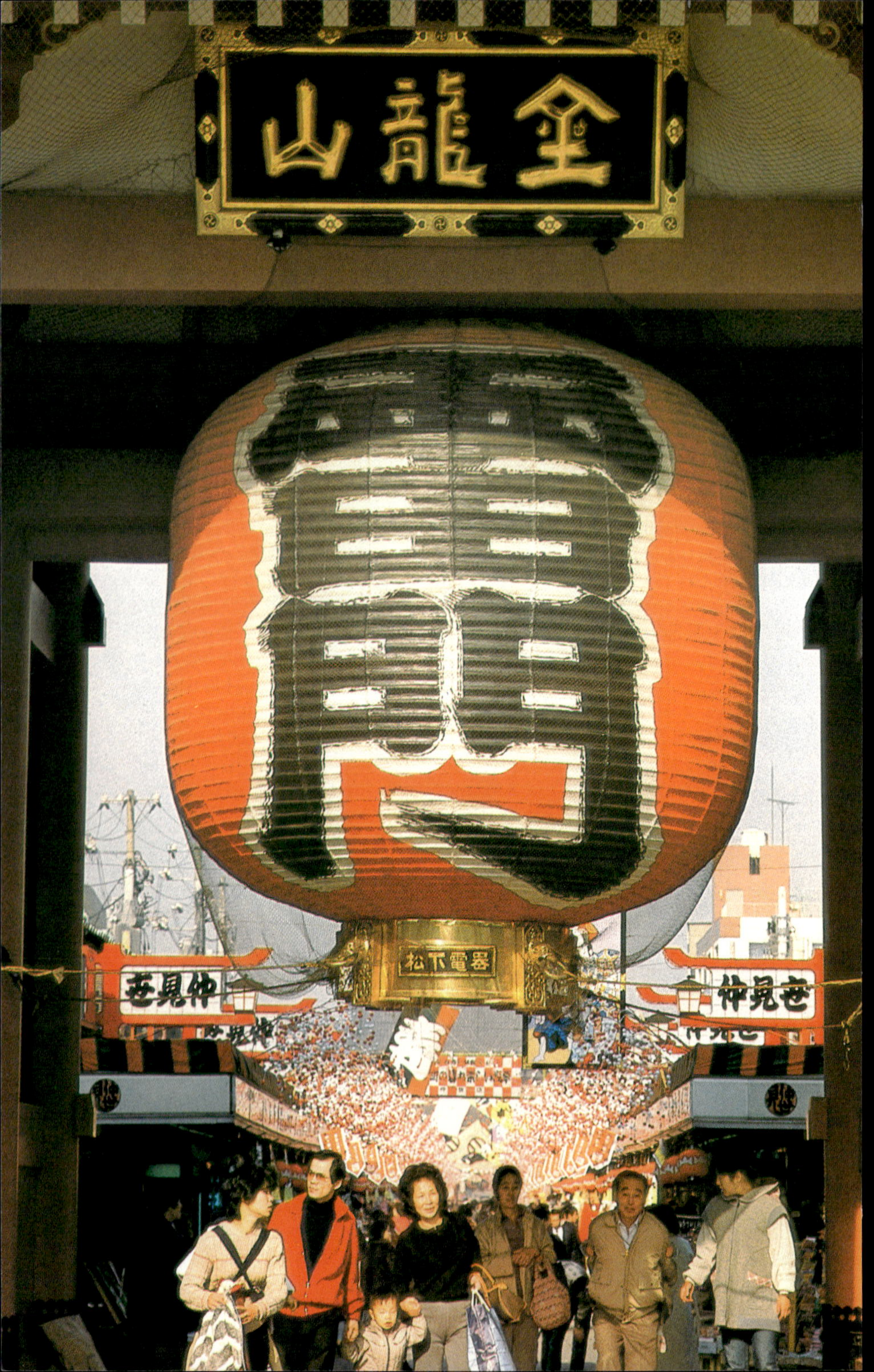
金龍山
雷門
松下電器
仲見世
仲見世

New Year firemen's festival, Kano Temple, Tokyo

for industrial air pollution in the city and more and more people began to question whether Tokyo was a fit place for the capital at all.

Since the end of the 1960s however the quality of life in the capital has gradually improved. The pollution problem has been basically overcome, helped by the relocation of much industry away from the centre of the city. At the same time, although the conurbation continues to expand, the population density of the inner city has been slowly decreasing.

Geography

If the layout of Tokyo seems incomprehensible, that is only partially because of its castle-town origins. There is also its transport system. Many years ago it was decided that only public bodies could build railways and subways in the city centre, while private companies could operate in the suburbs. These companies were dynamic and innovative. Having built their railways into places like Shinjuku, Ikebukuro and Shibuya, they then diversified into department stores and a whole lot of other enterprises in order to develop their inner suburban terminals into semi-independent cities rivalling the old-established central districts.

Today there are seven private railway companies and two public authorities (Japan National Railways and Metropolitan Bureau of Transport) running 40-odd train and subway lines, as well as the buses and one remaining streetcar line. Mostly unplanned, it is the finest transport system in the world; 23 million people use it every day.

The most celebrated trains are the pale green ones of the 22-mile (35 km) Yamanote (or Yamate) circle line. They are often recommended as the best way to see Tokyo (there is even a guidebook devoted to the subject, see Bibliography on page 120). The line has 29 stations, including the terminus-cities of the private railway companies.

Tokyo is a vast, time-consuming city. The visitor wishing to see the five main attractions of the city, starting from the Buddhist temple of Asakusa, via the National Museum of Ueno to the Imperial Palace Plaza to the National Diet, ending at the Emperor Meiji's Shrine, will cover about 7.5 miles (12 km). Doing the same thing in London, a large city with two historically distinct centres, would mean covering only about half as much ground (4.4 miles or 7 km to be precise, starting at the Tower and ending at Buckingham Palace). The figure for New York would only be a small fraction of that for Tokyo.

The heart of the capital is divided into three districts. Chiyoda, Chuo, and Minato wards, including the Imperial Palace, are called Central (Toshin). Taito, Sumida, and Koto wards are referred to as Downtown (Shitamachi), but not in the American sense: they are low-lying, traditional, poor sections of the old city. In contrast Uptown (Yamanote), the wards of Bunkyo, Toshima, Shinjuku, Shibuya, and Meguro, has much new postwar development in addition to its old areas. The Uptown population is typically young, fashionable and single: 37 percent of accommodation is occupied by people living alone.

Central

The Imperial Palace is like a great green lung in the middle of the grey city, but it is not the historical centre. In Tokugawa times all distances were computed from the north side of Nihombashi (the Bridge of Japan), which was first built in 1603. William Adams, the first Englishman to live in Japan (and hero of Clavell's *Shogun*), moved into a house nearby and the area used to be named after him. Today it is an interesting old part of the city with traditional-style Soba noodle houses and the head offices of long-established trading and industrial enterprises. It is best known for its department stores, Mitsukoshi and Takashimaya.

A little more than a mile (1.9 km) southwest of Nihombashi is the Imperial Palace Plaza with the most famous view of Tokyo: this is of the Nijubashi (Double Bridge), actually two bridges leading into the palace, one of stone and one of iron. The palace buildings were bombed during the war and rebuilt in 1968 in the western section of what was formerly Edo Castle. They are not open to the public, but it is possible to visit Kitanomaru (the Northern Keep) and the East Garden.

On the east side of the Imperial Palace is Marunouchi, the main business centre of Tokyo dignified by the old Dutch-style edifice of Tokyo

Station, built in 1914. To the south, on the other side of the railway tracks is Ginza, the most expensive, the smartest entertainment area of the capital, but now eclipsed by other localities as a shopping centre. Both Marunouchi and Ginza are laid out in parallel streets divided into neat rectangular blocks, of a kind only to be found on the eastern side of the Imperial Palace. Beyond Ginza is East Ginza, dominated by the Kabuki Theatre built in 'Momoyama style' in 1950, and then the interesting area of Tsukiji. Every morning the Tsukiji Wholesale Market provides Tokyo with its fish: the finest sushi houses of Japan are next to the market. The Tsukiji Honganji is probably the strangest Buddhist temple in the city. Built to be indestructible in 1935, it is in 'ancient Indian style'.

South of the Imperial Palace is the government area: the National Diet and the ministries of Nagatacho and Kasumigaseki. Near the Prime Minister's house, next to the Hilton Hotel, is the Hie Shrine, one of the oldest in Tokyo, but destroyed in the war. It was rebuilt in 1959. Further to the south is another entertainment area called Akasaka, which has a mixture of restaurants, night clubs, and sophisticated, exclusive geisha houses where top government and business leaders meet.

Further south again is Roppongi, originally a high class residential area with many embassies. It is now the favourite late night scene for young Tokyoites, the location of the discos, the place where foreign style is most enthusiastically emulated.

Northeast of the palace is Kudan and the Yasukuni Shrine. Marked by a huge bronze *torii* gate, Yasukuni is dedicated to all those who have given their lives in the service of Japan. It is famous for its springtime cherry blossoms and during the last war Japanese soldiers would pledge themselves 'to meet under the cherry trees of Kudan', which meant in death.

North of the palace are Kanda and then Hongo, both formerly wards. This is the university quarter, with rows and rows of bookshops and publishers' offices. The landmark of Kanda is the domed Greek Orthodox Nicolai Cathedral built in 1884 by a Russian priest. Hongo, at the point where Central, Uptown and Downtown meet, is an interesting traditional residential area with many old inns, chiefly used by children on school excursion trips to see the capital.

Downtown

The Downtown district is the home of the *Edokko*, Tokyo residents of three or more generations who maintain the traditions of the city and disdain the trendy Uptown parvenus of Shibuya and Meguro. Westerners who identify with places like Greenwich Village and Covent Garden will find it the most interesting section of the capital.

While there is a small Shitamachi (Downtown) Museum next to the pond in Ueno which is devoted to recording the life-style of local residents

Shinjuku skyline, Tokyo

in former times, the most typical part of the old Downtown is Koto Ward on the east side of the Sumida River. Seldom visited by foreigners, the ward has a high proportion of traditional wooden buildings. It is officially regarded as the most vulnerable part of Tokyo to earthquake, fire and flood damage. Since 1969 six special disaster prevention bases have been established in the ward.

In contrast to Koto, two areas of Taito are on every tour itinerary. Ueno Park has the capital's principal cultural complex including the Tokyo National Museum, the Tokyo Metropolitan Fine Art Gallery, the National Museum of Western Art, the Tokyo Metropolitan Festival Hall (where concerts are given), and Ueno Zoo as well as a number of shrines and temples. To the north is Yanaka, another interesting old residential area, known for its haunted cemeteries.

Asakusa on the west bank of the Sumida River was formerly the location of the Yoshiwara, the licensed brothel quarter put out of business by General MacArthur after the war. It is still an entertainment area that operates close to the law. Sensoji, popularly known as the Asakusa Kannon Temple, is the best-loved Buddhist establishment in the city. In 628 some fishermen found a small gold statue of the Bodhisattva Avalokitesvara (Kannon, in Japanese) and the temple was built near the spot. Destroyed in the war, it was rebuilt in 1958.

Koto accompaniment at a No *play, Tokyo*

Uptown

Though Shibuya is more fashionable and Ikebukuro more futuristic, Shinjuku remains the main sub-city of Uptown. With more neon and more noise than anywhere else in Tokyo, Shinjuku has three private railway terminals, two national railway lines and two subways, five department stores, and the largest complex of skyscrapers in the city. But it is becoming a business centre rather than the bohemian quarter it was in the 1960s (as depicted in Oshima Nagisa's 1969 film *Diary of a Shinjuku Thief*). It is no longer the place where coffee-shop intellectuals discuss revolution and bombs, and lady poetesses with red hair cultivate relationships with black American jazz musicians.

Shibuya to the south has only four department stores to boast of, but adjacent Harajuku is the most fashion-conscious place in Tokyo. Like Roppongi in Central, it is popular with young people who shop in the boutiques, relax in the coffee shops, and expend their energies in the discos. Nearby is the shrine dedicated to the Emperor Meiji (1852-1912), who presided over the first phase of the modernization of his country. (The shrine does not contain his grave.) Set in a beautiful park with a lovely iris garden, the shrine is the most important in Tokyo. It is an austere, quiet place in complete contrast to Harajuku.

Twenty years ago the elegant *Nagel's Encyclopedia-Guide Japan* gave this advice to anybody venturing to Ikebukuro: 'It is not advisable to explore the area beyond the west entry of the station at night, unless accompanied by a Japanese'. Times have changed and a safe Ikebukuro is becoming the most exciting Uptown centre of the 1980s. Much of this is due to the Seibu Company which runs a railway line, the largest department store in Japan, and a successful baseball team. The company exerts great influence on the life-style and leisure pursuits of young people throughout the country.

Yokohama

Yokohama is a major international port and an important section of the greater Tokyo conurbation. It is now the second largest city in Japan with a population of 2.83 million, having recently outstripped Osaka.

In the 1850s it was little more than a fishing village with a beach when it was adopted by western merchants as the site for a foreign settlement, in the aftermath of the epoch-making visit to Japan by Commodore Perry and a quarter of the American Navy. Perry had actually demonstrated his model railway to Japanese officials on Yokohama beach. Within 35 years it had turned into a city with 120,000 people.

Most of Yokohama was destroyed in the 1923 earthquake, and again by the air-raids at the end of the Second World War. In both cases the city was consumed by fire. Nevertheless some parts of the old Yokohama have survived in the area known as the 'Bluff' or Yamatemachi.

Yokohama today is a pleasant city, proud of its history, but for most foreign visitors the most interesting place in the city will be Sankeien. This is a fine landscaped park containing a collection of outstanding examples of traditional Japanese architecture, which have been moved to the site. The most impressive building is the villa of a feudal lord dating from the early Edo period which compares with the great Katsura Palace in Kyoto. There is also a magnificent high-roofed farmhouse, built in the 18th century in the mountains of Gifu Prefecture.

Kamakura

Kamakura was the *de facto* capital of Japan from 1192 to 1333, the first important city to be built in eastern Japan. It is now one of the three or four most frequently visited historic places in the country, with a legacy of 65-odd Buddhist temples and 20 Shinto shrines, and of course the celebrated bronze statue of the Great Buddha. Kamakura is only an hour from Tokyo on the southern edge of the commuter belt. It is a favourite residential area for well-to-do writers, artists, and foreigners. Located on Sagami Bay, south of Yokohama, it is a popular seaside resort as well as a sightseeing destination.

Kamakura symbolizes the decline of Kyoto in the 12th century and the rise of the military class known as *bushi* (warriors), or more commonly abroad, *samurai* (retainers). Intense rivalry developed between two factions of provincial military leaders in the 11th century. They were called the Minamoto and the Taira, both of imperial blood. One branch of the Minamoto established themselves in Kanto in the middle of the century. A civil war followed in the 12th century, won by the Taira who made a point of liquidating as many Minamoto as they could find. Uncharacteristically they spared two Minamoto children from the Kanto branch: Yoritomo (1147-1199) and his brother Yoshitsune (1159-1189). For the Taira this was a fatal mistake.

Yoritomo grew up in exile on the Izu Peninsula just west of Kamakura. He re-established Minamoto control over Kanto, made his headquarters at Kamakura in 1180 and revolted against the Taira. Yoshitsune led the Minamoto forces to the west, driving the Taira before him and finally annihilating them in 1185. The brothers then quarrelled leading to the death of Yoshitsune four years later. (The Japanese have always sympathized with the younger brother.)

In 1192 Yoritomo was given the old title of *Seii-tai-shogun* (Barbarian-quelling Generalissimo) formerly given to leaders fighting the Ainu. Shortened simply to *shogun*, Yoritomo was the first ruler of the feudal era to use the title. He died in 1199, leaving an even stronger personality in charge, his widow Masako. She succeeded in making her own family, the Hojo, the real rulers of Japan during the rest of the Kamakura period which lasted till 1333. Political power then went back to Kyoto, while Kamakura was made the administrative centre of eastern Japan from 1336 to 1573, after which it declined into little more than a fishing town.

Kamakura today is a city of festivals. Many of them recall the early history of the city. At the beginning of April each year there is a costume pageant led through the city by Yoritomo in full 12th-century armour. In mid-September there is a horseback archery contest with competitors in samurai dress of the Kamakura period. This is held at the Hachiman Shrine, founded by an early Minamoto leader in 1063 and rebuilt by Yoritomo in 1180. The God of War, Hachiman, was the patron deity of the Minamoto family. Within the shrine there is a famous dance pavilion where Shizuka, the mistress of Yoshitsune, was compelled to dance against her will for the pleasure of Yoritomo.

According to legend it was Yoritomo himself who first considered dedicating a great Buddha at Kamakura, but it was not cast until half a century later in 1252. Like the other great, bronze Buddha at Nara, it was originally housed in a large wooden hall, but this was destroyed in 1495. The figure is of the Amida Buddha (Amitabha) and is 37 foot (11.4 metres) tall. The Great Buddha is seated with his hands in a gesture expressing faith.

Archery festival, Tsurugaka, Kamakura

Hakone

The Hakone district, in the extreme southwest corner of Kanto, is the major resort of the region. It is part of the Fuji-Hakone-Izu National Park (for which see also page 41). It can be reached in about an hour and a half from Tokyo's Odakyu Shinjuku Railway Station and makes a pleasant day trip from the capital.

During Tokugawa times Hakone was the main checkpoint on the road between Edo (now Tokyo) and Kyoto, when the shogunate imposed strict controls on the activities, and movements, of the feudal lords. Foreigners discovered the district about the time of the Meiji Restoration. One venerable old European-style hotel remains at Miyanoshita. It is called the Fujiya and was built in 1878.

The Hakone district lies within the large crater of an extinct volcano. It is 25 miles (40 km) in circumference, with a lake called Ashi curving around the southwest rim of the crater. There are several peaks in the centre of which the highest is 4,718 feet (1,438 metres) high. There are numerous, well-patronized hot springs, however the crowning glory of Hakone is the view of Japan's best-loved mountain, Fuji.

Nikko

Nikko National Park is on the northern edge of the Kanto Plain, within a couple of hours of Tokyo by train. Millions of visitors come each year, not

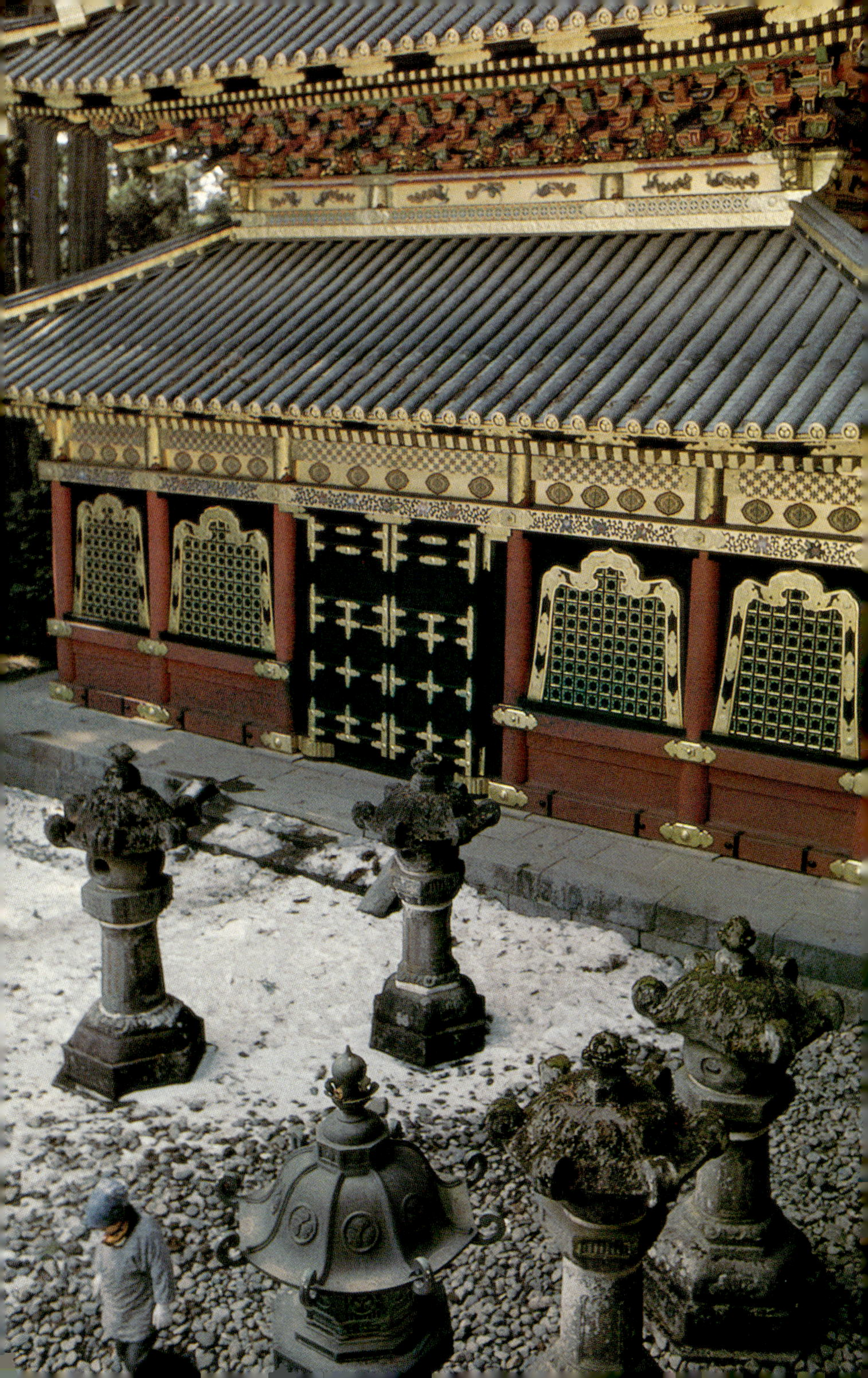

to see the lakes, waterfalls and high mountains (all attractive enough in themselves), but the mausoleums of the last ruling family of feudal Japan, the Tokugawa. In particular they come to see the extravagantly decorated shrine, and austere tomb of Tokugawa Ieyasu (1542-1616), the first shogun of his line.

Ieyasu came to power at the end of the most exuberant and colourful period of Japanese history, the Azuchi-Momoyama (1573-1603), named after the great castle on Lake Biwa built by Oda Nobunaga (1534-1582) and the sumptuous palace erected in Kyoto by Hideyoshi (1536-1598). These two generals in succession tried to unify Japan. Imperious, ambitious men (Hideyoshi wanted to invade China) they achieved some successes but were unable to pass on power to their heirs; Azuchi Castle and Momoyama Palace no longer exist. Ieyasu, popularly called the 'old racoon dog', a tribute to his deceitfulness, had his opportunity and took it, seizing power from the heir of Hideyoshi and succeeding in founding a dynasty. His great memorial *does* still exist, at Nikko.

Several temples near the small town of Nikko were founded in the 8th century though nothing now remains that is earlier than the 17th century. The site attracted the attention of Ieyasu and he left instructions that he should be buried there. His body was brought in 1617, a year after his death. He received the posthumous title of Tosho Daigongen or 'East Illuminating Incarnation' (of a bodhisattva). The buildings in front of his tomb are called the Toshogu, or 'East Illuminating Shrine'.

The shrine to be seen today was built under the orders of Iemitsu, the third shogun and grandson of Ieyasu. He employed 15,000 workmen and artisans, most of them from Kyoto, who managed to complete their work in only two years starting in 1634.

No expense was spared. The Toshogu is in spectacular Momoyama style rather than the more restrained taste of the Edo period (1603-1868). Acres of gold leaf were used to embellish the buildings. Large contributions were exacted from the feudal lords as part of a policy of keeping them subservient to the shogunate. One relatively poor lord contributed thousands of Japanese cedar saplings, which today are magnificent trees towering over the various buildings. The Toshogu was well endowed in order to guarantee its maintenance. Restoration work has been going on almost continuously since the 17th century.

The shrine dedicated to Ieyasu consists of various gates, storehouses, a library, stables, a pagoda, bell and drum towers, and a sacred palanquin house in front of the main halls of the complex where Ieyasu is enshrined with Hideyoshi and Minamoto Yoritomo. The inner halls are very elaborate but the most popular part of the complex is the Yomeimon, or Gate of Sunlight, an ornately carved and decorated two-storey structure, primarily in white and gold.

The tomb of Ieyasu is on a hill behind the main buildings of the shrine. It is in the shape of a small bronze pagoda dating from 1683 when the original stone one was damaged by an earthquake. During the Edo period it could only be visited by specially designated officials, once every 50 years.

Mashiko

The town of Mashiko is celebrated for its pottery. Located only 60 miles (95 km) north of Tokyo, the local industry dates back to the mid-19th century. It was discovered in the 1930s by Hamada Shoji (1894-1978), a great potter and folk art enthusiast. The English ceramist Bernard Leach lived and worked in the town for a number of years, helping later to establish Mashiko's international reputation.

Hamada's home, workshop and kiln are open to the public. The Mashiko Reference Collection Museum contains pottery and other pieces of folk art, collected by Hamada from all over the world. There are also examples of his own work. The museum is housed in two fine old stone storehouses, built in the traditional local style. Hamada's workshop complete with its row of potter's wheels, is austere and simple, one of a group of old, wooden, thatched buildings originally bought by the potter and re-erected on his land at Mashiko.

The town now has 60-odd kilns, and almost as many shops. Produced entirely with local materials, the pottery of Mashiko has become very popular. Although it is on sale in Tokyo and elsewhere, many people still come to the town to hunt for particularly fine pieces.

Northeast Honshu (Tohoku)

If Michinoku (paths deep in the interior) is the old name for the northeast of Honshu, that is still how most Japanese think of it today — the back of beyond. It was the last part of the main island to be claimed by the people we now call the Japanese. There are still faint reminders, particularly in the place names, of the Ainu who lived in Tohoku before being driven back to the northern island of Hokkaido.

Communications have never been good in the northeast. An almost unbroken line of mountains divides the region from north to south. The prefectures of Yamagata and Akita on the west Japan Sea coast have their own special characters in contrast to those of Fukushima, Miyagi and Iwate prefectures on the Pacific side. The difference is more a matter of climate than separate traditions. The Japan Sea coast is more humid than the Pacific, and in the winter it has much more snow. At one time the west coast ports traded with Kyoto and Osaka by sea and at that time were considered more sophisticated than the east. But today all the main lines of

Matsushima, northeast Honshu

communication run through the eastern cities of Fukushima, Sendai and Morioka and that is where economic development is concentrated.

The character of Tohoku has much in common with the central mountainous area of Honshu with which it once formed a common unit called Tosando. Like Chubu, Tohoku offers much for the adventurous visitor with plenty of time. Travellers interested in the land, the people and the old values of Japanese society will find much to experience in Tohoku. There are few historical sites in this part of Japan, and also fewer tourists.

Sendai and Matsushima

Sendai is the principal city of northeast Honshu. It was destroyed by fire-bombs in the last war and has been rebuilt as a modern city with wide, tree-lined avenues. This is evidence of planning rarely found in other Japanese cities, certainly not in Tokyo. The population of Sendai is over 600,000.

Date Masamune (1566-1636), founder of the city and the first major leader of the northeast after the Fujiwara of Hiraizumi, is omnipresent: almost everything worth seeing in the area is connected with him. He was a remarkable man, best known for sending one of his retainers, Hasekura Tsunenaga, on a mission to the Vatican.

The awesome foundations of the castle that Date Masamune built in 1602 are still to be seen on a hill overlooking the city, though the

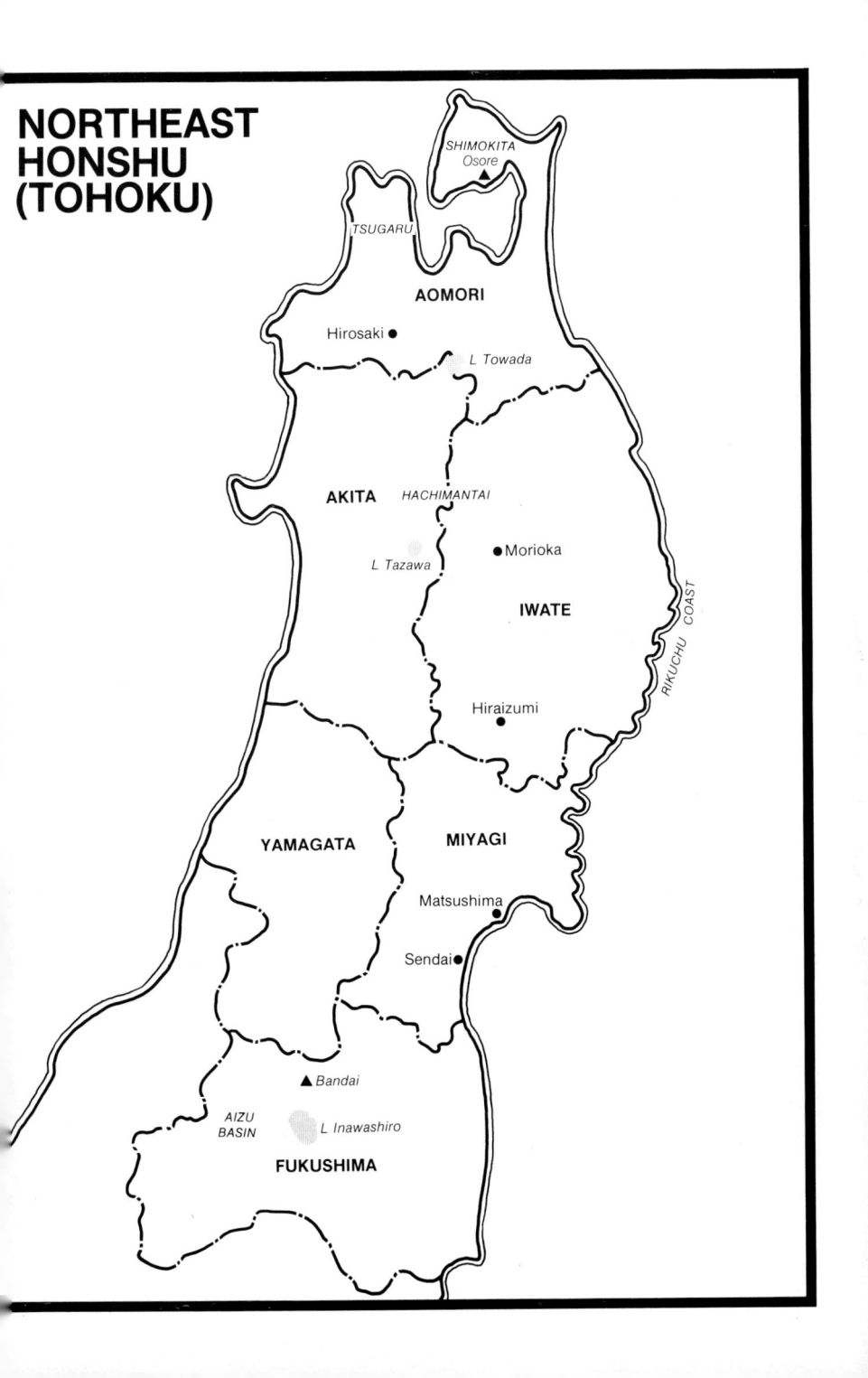

NORTHEAST HONSHU (TOHOKU)

superstructure was demolished in 1875 after the rule of the Date family had been ended by the new Tokyo-based government of the Emperor Meiji. The mausoleum of Date Masamune was destroyed in the war, but a replica has been built in sumptuous Momoyama style. There is also a fine Shinto shrine called Osaki Hachiman built by Date Masamune in 1607.

Just an hour from Sendai by road is Matsushima, which together with Miyajima and Amanohashidate is designated one of the 'three most beautiful views' in the country. The celebrated *haiku* poet Basho (1644-1694) thought it unrivalled. There are 260 white sandstone and volcanic tuff islands within Matsushima Bay, carved by the sea into an endless variety of shapes and surmounted by red and black pine trees, blown by prevailing sea breezes into a series of irregular forms. Visitors often take sightseeing boats around the bay, but the best views are still from old-established vantage points around the bay. The Matsushima dawn is incomparable.

Aizu Basin and Mount Bandai

A hundred miles (160 km) due north of Tokyo is the fertile Aizu Basin, divided from the Kanto Plain by a range of high mountains. For the foreigner the basin comes close to being a microcosm of Japan itself.

During the Tokugawa period (1603-1868) it was the key strategic area of the northeast and accordingly placed under the control of a branch of the ruling family. In 1868, during the last stand of the shogunate against the imperial restoration, the city of Aizu (now Aizu Wakamatsu) held out staunchly for the Tokugawa and was destroyed for its pains. The castle was demolished, the capital of the new prefecture moved to Fukushima, and many of the samurai exiled to the Shimokita Peninsula.

Today the people of Aizu Wakamatsu are proud of the history of their city, though considered self-willed and distrustful of outsiders. Few are able or willing to trace their families back to the period before the imperial restoration, though traditions of the feudal period are still alive, notably in the lacquer industry. The city was not bombed during the last war and is an attractive place, somewhat enhanced by the castle rebuilt in 1965, with an elegant hot spring resort called Higashiyama on its periphery.

On the opposite side of the basin from its main city is the old merchant town of Kitakata. A quiet, peaceful place producing the finest sake, soy sauce, fermented bean paste *(miso)*, and lacquerware while storing and distributing the area's high quality rice, Kitakata is one of the best places in Japan to see *kura* (storehouse) architecture. In contrast to light, woodframed typical Japanese houses, the kura have massive mud-lined walls with small windows. While designed for storage, many of those in Kitakata are residential.

North of the basin are the three sections of the magnificent Bandai-Asahi National Park. The nearest section to Aizu Wakamatsu is dominated by Bandai volcano, 5,968 feet high (1,819 metres). The mountainscape to be seen today has only existed since 1888 when a massive eruption caused by steam pressure (not lava) blew off an enormous chunk of the north side of Mount Bandai. Over 450 people died. A series of plateau lakes formed, with different coloured waters (due to mineral deposits), around which there is now one of the finest nature trails in the country.

Hiraizumi

Hiraizumi, unique in Tohoku, is of national historical importance: the Konjikido mausoleum at the Tendai Buddhist Chusonji is the most impressive monument in northern Japan.

Hiraizumi is located in a flat area of Iwate Prefecture where the Kitakami Basin opens out onto the plain of Sendai. Gold was discovered nearby and the district became a grand outpost of Heian culture from the end of the 11th century under the leadership of four generations of a family called Fujiwara. Their flourishing state came to an abrupt end after only a century. Minamoto Yoshitsune (1159-1189), the romantic fugitive brother of the Shogun Yoritomo sought refuge in the northeast from his brother's jealousy. At first the Fujiwara helped him, but later they betrayed and killed him. Immediately afterwards Yoritomo suppressed the Fujiwara.

The Konjikido (Golden Hall, or Hall of Light) exemplifies the grandeur of the Fujiwara of the northeast. It is not large, about 18 feet (5.5 metres) square, but decorated in a dazzling combination of gold, black lacquer and mother-of-pearl. A bold, unorthodox conception, the mummified remains of three of the Fujiwara (and the head of a fourth) are laid beneath a dais on top of which there are a series of statues of the deities of the Pure Land of the West, the Buddhist paradise, a symbol of the success of the Fujiwara in the afterlife. The Kojikido was built between 1109 and 1124. The Motsuji, another Buddhist establishment which is nearby, has a large garden dating back to the time of the Fujiwara rulers. This garden too represents the Pure Land.

Rikuchu Coast

Rikuchu is the old name for Iwate Prefecture, though the coastline named after it extends south into Miyagi Prefecture. Much of the Rikuchu coast is designated as a national park in recognition of the outstanding beauty of the rocky, indented shoreline bordering the Pacific Ocean. The national park extends 110 miles (180 km) from north to south and is of interest for its flora and fauna as well as its scenery.

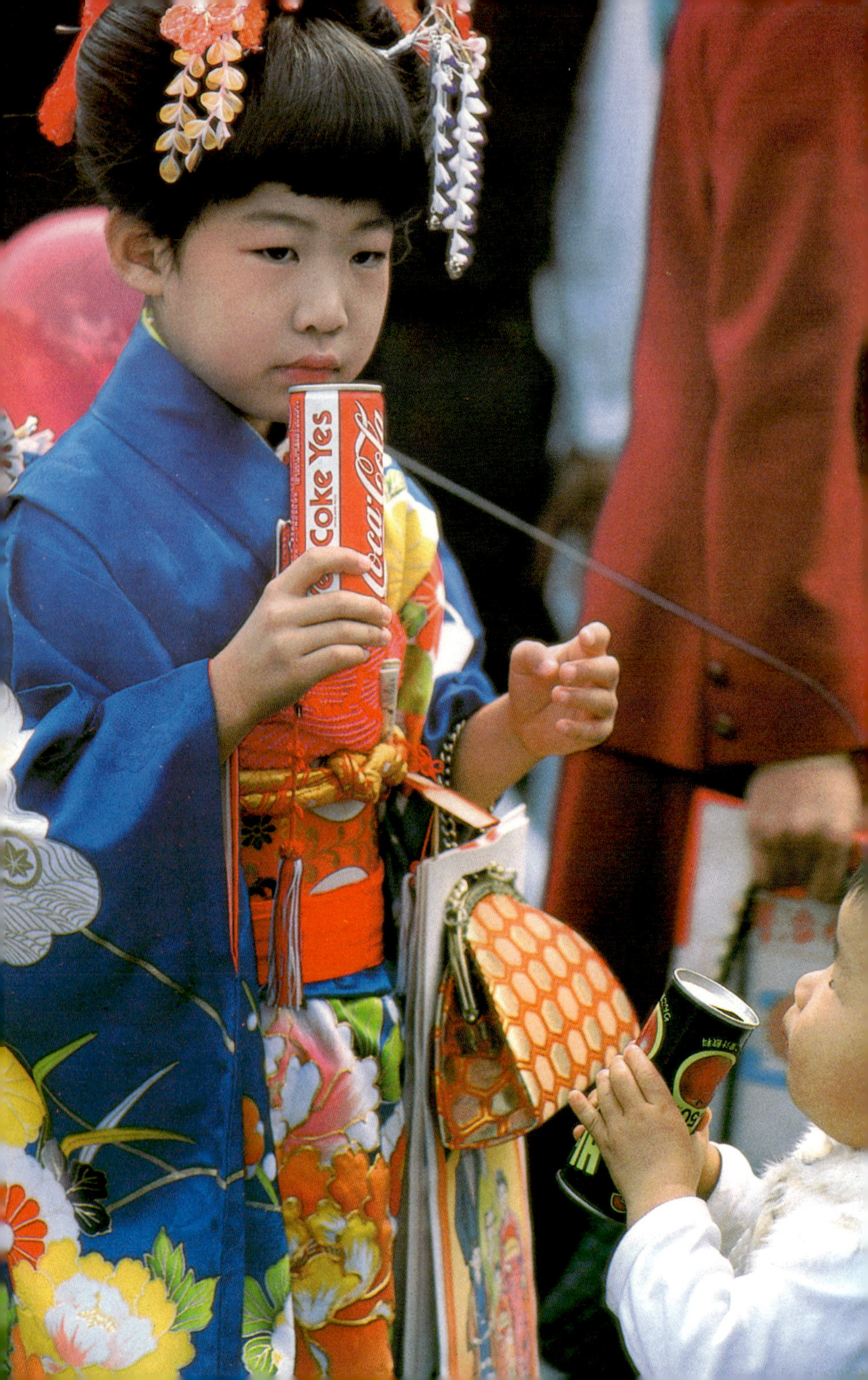
Coke Yes

In the centre is a fishing town called Miyako. This is where the principal attraction of the coast is located. Jodogahama, the 'Beach of the Pure Land' (of Buddhism), is a white pebbled strand facing across water to a line of white rocks surmounted by gnarled pines silhouetted against the sky. Incomparable at dawn or dusk, Jodogahama has all the perfection of a Zen garden in Kyoto, but on a grander scale.

Miyako effectively divides the coastline into two stretches, both of which are best seen by boat which can be taken from Miyako between the months of April and November. The northern section has impressive lines of cliffs, while the southern section is a *rias* type of submerged coast.

Morioka

Morioka was 'discovered' by the Japanese travelling public in 1982, when the city became the new northern terminus of the 'Bullet Train' Tohoku Shinkansen. However Morioka has a definite style and vigour of its own and is beginning to be recognized as a destination in its own right, rather than just a transit point for the open spaces of the region.

Originally the castle town of the Nambu lords, it retains the impressive foundations of the fortress as well as some of the traditions of the feudal period. Austerely beautiful hand-cast ironware, called *Nambu tekki*, is still made for use in Japan's formal tea ceremony. The ironware, mostly in the form of kettles, is the finest of its kind in Japan. It is still manufactured in small family-run workshops, located behind old shopfronts in the centre of the city, as it has been for generations.

Morioka is surrounded by superlatively beautiful countryside. To the northwest is Mount Iwate, a dormant conical volcano 6,696 feet high (2,041 metres), while in the opposite direction is the craggy Hayachine, famous for its wild alpine flowers, which is 6,279 feet high (1,914 metres). Beyond Hayachine is the Tono Basin, celebrated for its folk tales and picturesque thatched farmhouses.

Hachimantai Plateau, Lake Tazawa and Lake Towada

The central northern part of Tohoku has some of the most outstanding scenery in Japan, located in and around the Towada-Hachimantai National Park. The lava plateau of Hachimantai is popular for skiing and hiking. There is a profusion of natural hot springs. In one particularly spectacular area of geysers, solfataras, boiling lakes and mud volcanoes there are two old-fashioned resorts called Goshogake and Tamagawa. Offering either inn-style or dormitory (self catering) accommodation, they have old wooden bath houses complete with a series of different pools, water shoots, sauna and steam boxes. Mixed bathing is customary.

South of Hachimantai is the caldera lake of Tazawa. Quite round, its crater shape is easily apparent. Only 12 miles (20 km) in circumference, it is the deepest in Japan (1,394 feet or 425 metres) and never freezes in winter. It is a beautiful sight from the high plateau area above the lake.

To the north of Hachimantai is the double caldera Lake Towada, which is about twice the size of Tazawa. For Japanese tourists Towada is probably the most popular attraction in the whole of the region. They particularly appreciate the red and gold colours of autumn in the woods around the lake.

Hirosaki and Tsugaru Peninsula

Hirosaki is the main city on the western side of Aomori, the prefecture facing the island of Hokkaido across the Tsugaru Strait. It was formerly the headquarters of the lords of Tsugaru who ruled the area during the whole Tokugawa period from 1603 to 1868. Unlike the prefectural capital, Aomori City, it was spared American bombs during the last war and it remains the most pleasant medium-sized city to visit in the Tohoku region.

Hirosaki is known for its cherry trees, which are concentrated around the site of the old castle, where some of the old gates and a fine three-storeyed watch-tower are still standing. The cherry blossoms are the occasion of a local festival at the end of April and the beginning of May.

There are many other attractions, ranging from the city's old architecture and arts and crafts to the view of Mount Iwaki, a nearby dormant volcano 5,331 feet high (1,625 metres). The lower slopes of Hirosaki are girdled by apple orchards for which Aomori is also famous. But most foreign visitors will enjoy most of all the quiet, civilized, friendly atmosphere of the city itself, evidenced by its well-stocked bookshops, Tokyo-style classical music coffee shops, the gentle, lilting local dialect and the remarkable fact that the Tourist Information Office, by the station, rents out bicycles.

Beyond Hirosaki stretches the Tsugaru Peninsula with some of the most attractive and least-visited fishing villages in Japan. The peninsula ends at Cape Tappi, itself the starting point for the 34 mile (54 km) **Seikan** undersea tunnel to Hokkaido. Due to open in 1987, it will be the longest tunnel in the world.

Mount Osore and Shimokita Peninsula

Shimokita is the most northerly section of the main island, also the least touched by the hand of man. On the western side of the peninsula there are few settlements and only unsurfaced roads which have been built by Japan's Self Defence Force, the army. The most notable inhabitants are colonies of wild monkeys, found further north than anywhere else in the world. But if Shimokita is the last place on Honshu, its best-known landmark, Mount Osore, is more often thought of as the last place on earth. Osore, 'Mount Dread' in English, is in the centre of the peninsula not far from the city of Mutsu. The name refers to a crater area surrounded by eight volcanoes, in the middle of which is a lake. While the volcanoes themselves are apparently dormant, the whole crater area is alive with the effects of subterranean activity. Steaming, bubbling geysers and solfataras have created a multi-coloured, mineral-encrusted landscape almost devoid of vegetation.

If Osore offers a landscape of awesome desolation to the foreign visitor, to the Japanese it is the beginning of the land of the dead. The sacred temple called the Entsuji, on the north side of the lake, is said to date back to the 9th century, and the Buddhism it represents is of a primitive kind. Every year from the 20th to the 24th of July, blind women mediums from all over Tohoku gather at Osore to communicate with the dead on behalf of bereaved relatives.

Pilgrims also come at other times of the year to build up small piles of stones (to help lost souls on their way to paradise) and put fresh clothes on the innumerable stone statues of the Jizo (guardians of the frontier between this world and the next, patron deities of stillborn infants, children, travellers, and the dead). They stay at the temple inn and bathe in the hot spring bath house attached to it.

From the gate of the Entsuji the pilgrims can look down, past a red wooden bridge, to a double line of stakes disappearing from the shore into the middle of the lake. Along this passage flows the river of life itself, from this world — to the next.

Central Honshu (Chubu)

The island of Honshu's central region, a sizeable chunk of land including nine prefectures which stretch from the Pacific coast north across the Japan Alps to the Japan Sea, holds more for the traveller interested in traditional Japan than perhaps any other area in the country except the northeast of the island. The region has picturesque villages of thatched-roof houses, pine-framed seascapes, rugged mountains and some of the country's best folk art and festivals.

The chief cities are Nagoya, Kanazawa and Matsumoto. Nagoya, the nation's fourth largest metropolis, makes a convenient base for touring the area. Kanazawa, untouched by the Second World War, may be Japan's best preserved castle town, though the castle itself has gone. Matsumoto's castle still stands and is one of the country's most dramatic.

The traveller serious about seeing the real Japan will want to venture further into the Japan Alps, either from Takayama, with its old wooden houses and shops, or from Matsumoto to Kamikochi or Hirayu Onsen, two high-altitude spots completely surrounded by tall mountains.

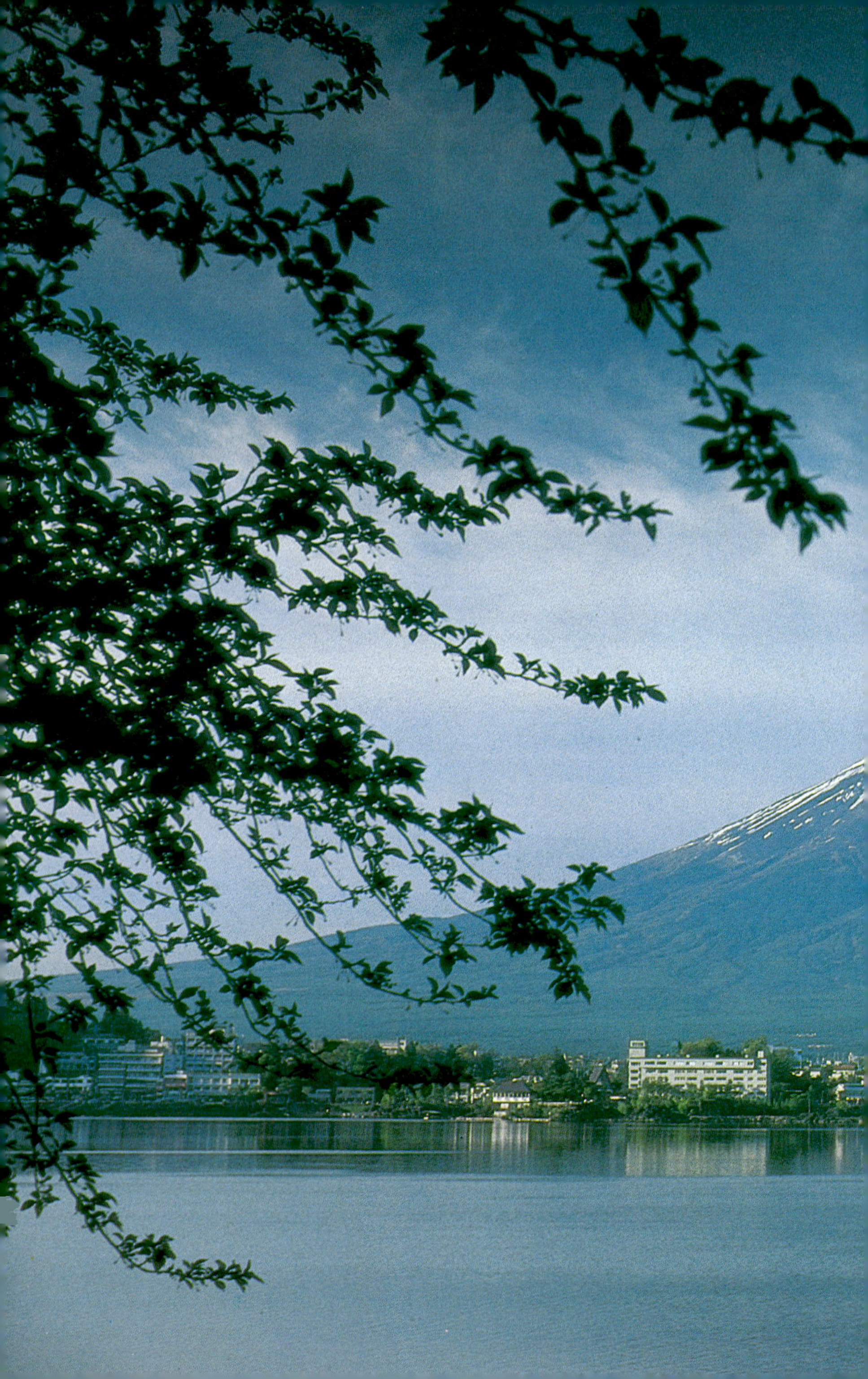

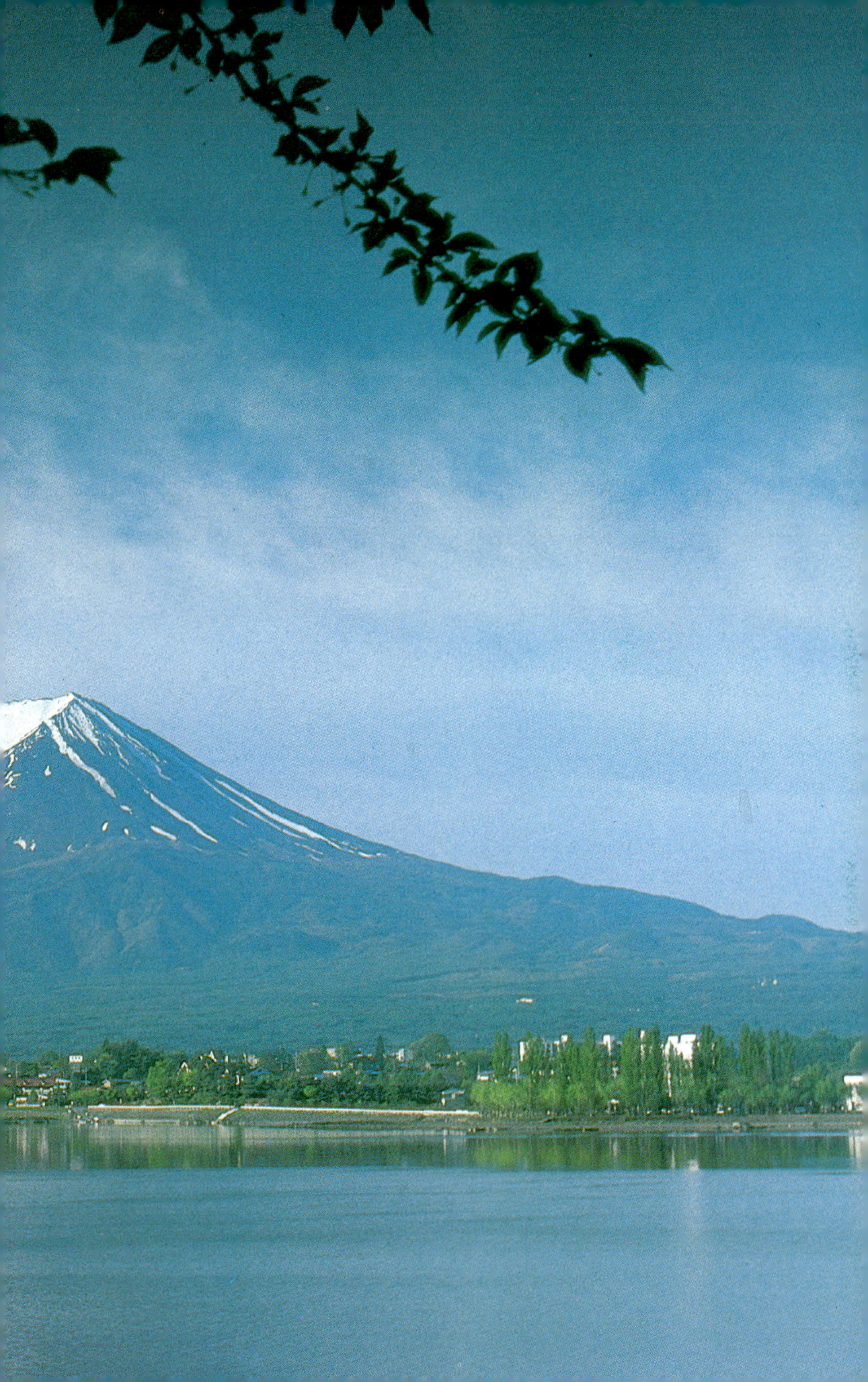

Mount Fuji

As fascinating to Japanese as it is to foreigners, the sacred mountain is an apt and enduring symbol, with its tranquil beauty, long periods of calm, and occasional violent eruptions, of the Japanese nation itself.

You can sometimes see Fuji-san (the *san* here means, disappointingly, mountain and not mister) from central Tokyo, if you select a high vantage spot and look in the direction marked by the skyscrapers of Shinjuku. Weather permitting, you should see Fuji's matchless cone floating above the horizon to the west. Dusk is the best time in summer, and in winter very early in the morning, when the air is clearest and the sun first strikes Fuji's snowy mantle.

This glimpse seldom fails to provoke a desire to see the fabled mountain closer up. The 'Bullet Train' to Nagoya or Kyoto gives quite a good view of Fuji, the Chuo and Tomei Expressways, running respectively north and south of the mountain, even better ones. In winter this is about as close as you can get; the pine forests on Fuji's lower slopes are smothered in snow, and the cone above the treeline, constantly swept by avalanches, is far too dangerous to climb.

In summer, and especially in the blessed months of July and August (the official season for climbing Fuji) you can come as close as you please, even to the crater on the summit. Some two million Japanese climb at least part-way up Fuji every year. Approaching by train to Kawaguchiko (one of Fuji's five lakes) on the northern side, or the quiet country town of Gotemba on the southern, you go thence by bus to the Fifth Station or, from the Gotemba side, the New Fifth Station. At both of these places, each about 7,000 feet (2,000 metres) in altitude, you can purchase a wooden climbing stick, a conical straw hat, beer, soft drinks and provisions for the climb.

There are five more stations (actually clusters of huts built of stone, wire and corrugated iron) to go to the summit, 12,388 feet (or 3,776 metres). Wear strong shoes or boots, as there is some rough scrambling, although no actual climbing. Along the way you can purchase refreshments and space to rest, the prices growing steeper as the mountain does, with a current peak of ¥2,500 to lie on a straw mat for a few hours, under a quilt-like *futon*, out of the piercing wind, to wait for the spectacular sunrise and unforgettable view from the summit.

Nagoya and the Pacific Coast

Now a city of over 2 million people, Nagoya is almost synonymous with Japan's industrial success in recent times. The undoubted centre of the

CENTRAL HONSHU (CHUBU)

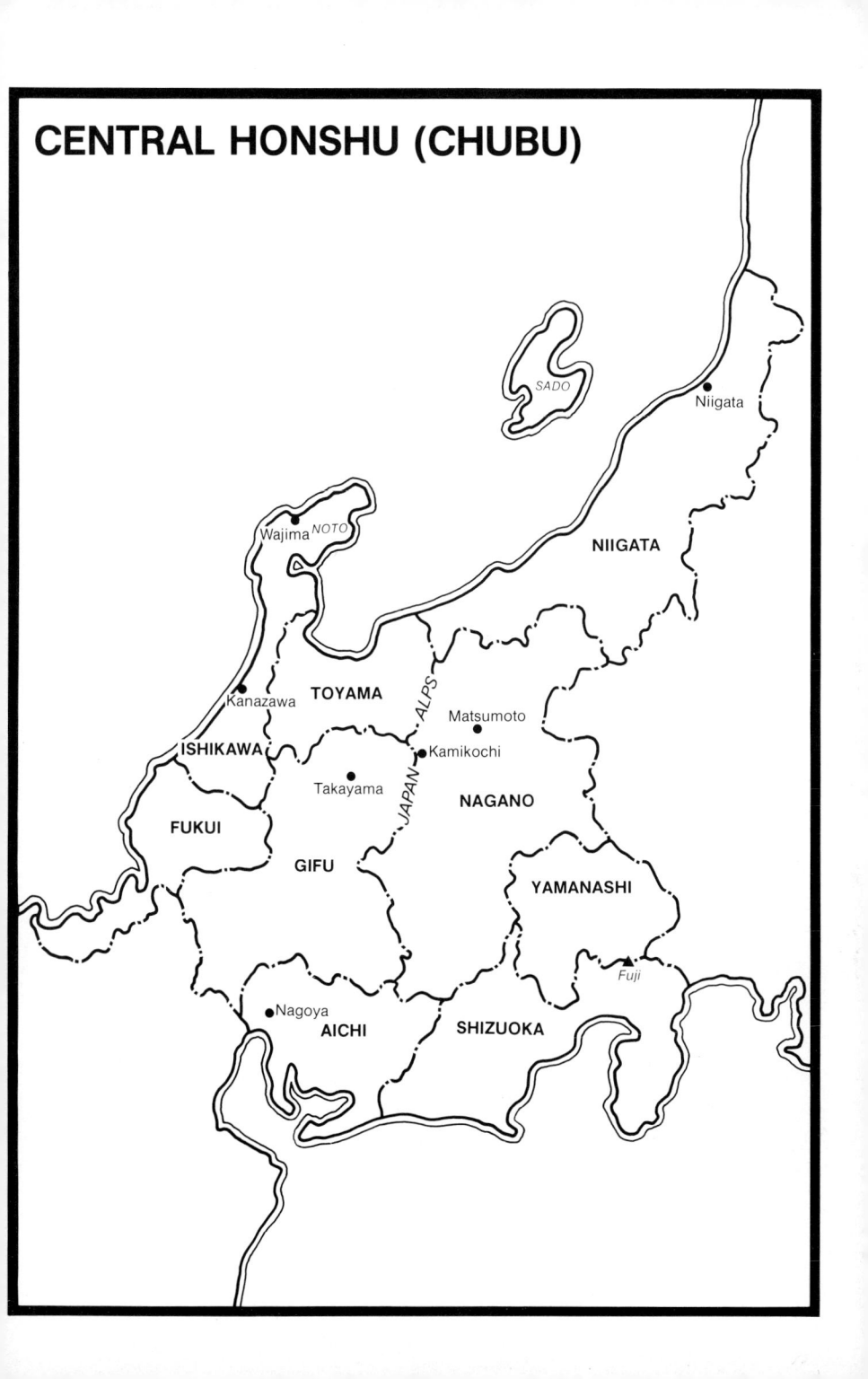

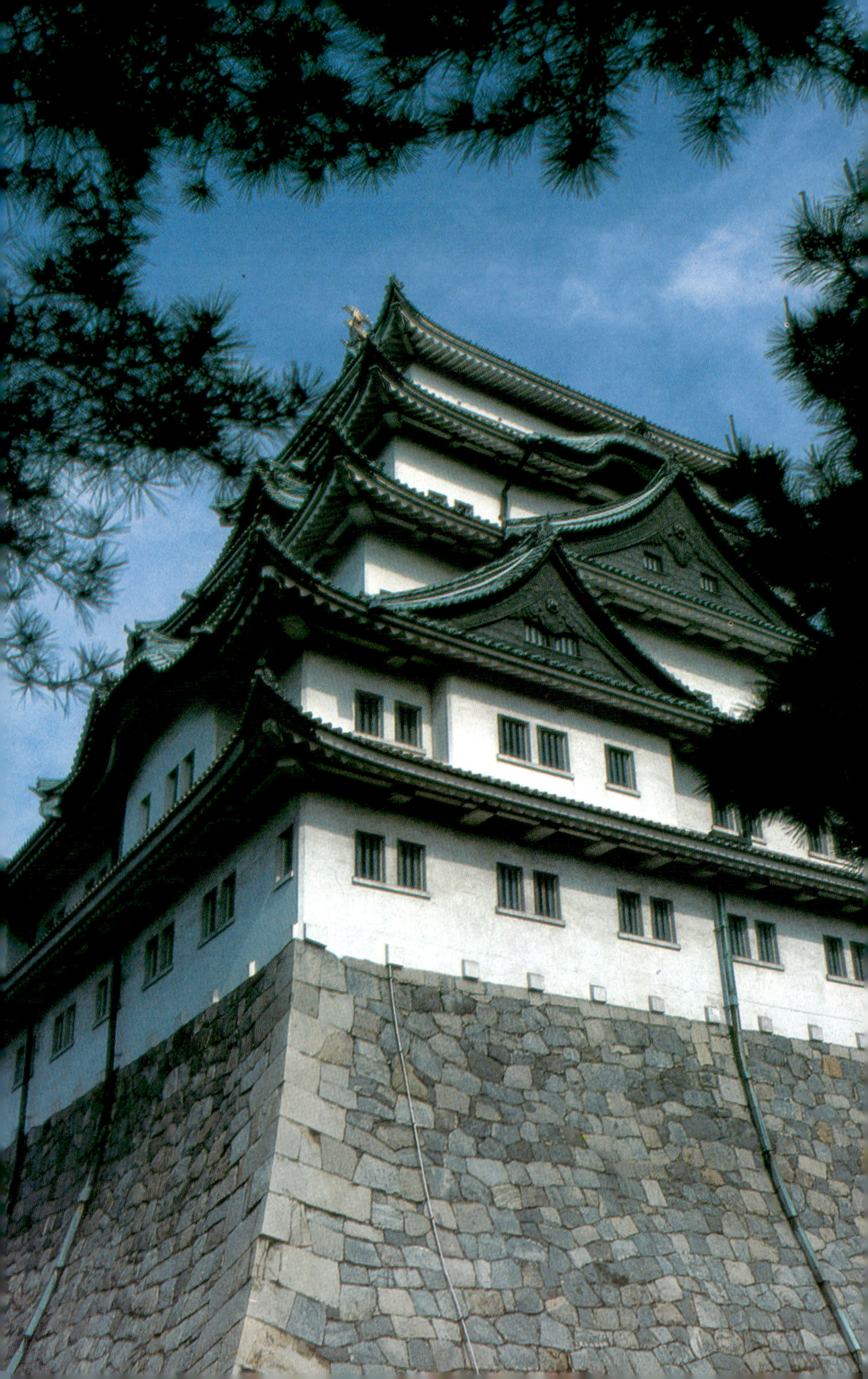

Japanese car industry, it is a focus of futuristic manufacturing technologies including robots, electronics, and new materials.

Reached by bullet train, the appropriate way to get to such a hothouse of innovation, Nagoya is unmistakably a working city. But it contains many places of interest such as its fine castle, built by the Shogun Tokugawa Ieyasu (1542-1616). The Noritake china company and the pearl industry of Ise Bay also uses Nagoya as a showplace.

The surrounding land is distinctive for its steep forest-covered mountains and deep coastal indentations. On the Kiso River, a ride through the rapids is breathtaking. On the nearby Nagara River, fishermen use cormorants to catch sweetfish during the summer months. Numerous hot spring resorts offer relaxation after walks along mountain trails.

Kanazawa

Although there is nothing left of the castle that dominated this castle town, there is still enough character left around the fortress to stir the imagination about what life must have been like during the country's austere feudal period.

This was no ordinary castle town. It was ruled by the Maeda clan of feudal lords, quite probably the most powerful group of despots aside from the shoguns themselves during the long Edo Period (1603-1868). Since the Tokugawa clan in Edo, being the ever-paranoid rulers that they were, constantly expected trouble from the Maeda, and the Maeda, likewise, were suspicious of the shogunate, Kanazawa was built for possible battle with narrow, winding streets to slow down an attack, temples strategically placed on the east side of the Sai River from which the enemy was expected to approach, and even an escape hatch for the ruling lord cleverly concealed under a temple named Myoritsuji (more commonly known as Ninjadera or Spy Temple).

More than just tyrants, the Maeda had taste as evidenced by the city's most famous attraction, Kenroku Garden. It ranks as one of Japan's three great stroll gardens. Seisonkaku Villa, once home to the mother of the 13th Maeda lord, and the Ishikawa Prefectural Art Museum, with its permanent collection of the city's most famous product, Kutani ceramics, are both adjacent to the garden.

There are also a number of small, private museums and a quarter full of samurai houses to complete the picture of life in a feudal castle town. The Honda Museum, a short walk from the art museum, houses the family treasures of the chief advisers of the Maeda. The Nagamachi district, steps from the shopping area, offers a glimpse of the era's stoic style with mud walls topped with grey tile, and the Saihitsuan Yuzen Silk Centre where designs painted on Kanazawa's famous silk are displayed.

Noto Peninsula and Wajima

The Noto Peninsula bends out into the Sea of Japan like a finger beckoning to Asia. During the Nara Period (645-794), its towns grew up as important way points for trade with the continent. But trade routes shifted and as land routes to the area were few and difficult, the Noto became a backwater in the stream of Japanese history that retained customs which changed or died out elsewhere.

Remnants of the once all-powerful Taira clan fled to this isolated area in 1186 after their disastrous defeat by the Minamoto, bringing with them the customs and culture of the capital. Several Edo Period houses built by descendants of the Taira and other prosperous clans preserve the style of the farming and merchant life of the Noto people of three hundred years ago.

Wajima, the largest town in the upper peninsula, is divided by a river into two distinct parts. Fishermen and divers live on one side and the artisans who work in Wajima's famous lacquer industry live on the other. The morning market is very old and as much a social occasion as a commercial one. Women from town, from outlying farms and fisherwomen gather to buy and sell fresh produce. Lightly salted and steamed abalone is a Wajima product known throughout Japan.

Pieces of lacquerware made in the Heian Period have been found in Wajima, and the lacquer tree brought from China grows well in the hills surrounding the town. Wajima lacquerware can be very expensive as it is usually made to order and is very strong. Fine examples are on display in stores in the lacquer makers' part of town.

Agriculture, fishing and diving are the mainstays of Noto life, and women dominate them. Women vendors criss-cross the peninsula daily by train and bus bartering, buying and selling goods. Women are also divers, and the birth of a girl to a fisherman's family is celebrated as the birth of a boy would be elsewhere in Japan.

An hour's bus ride southwest of Wajima is the old town of Monmae which grew up around the monastery of Sojiji built in 1321. The Noto became a bastion of the Soto School of Zen Buddhism, and though fires have taken their toll of the Sojiji's buildings, the monastery and the town still evoke feelings of the Kamakura Period.

Niigata and Sado Island

The sprawling city of Niigata, the largest port on the Japan Sea coast, is very heavily industrialized. In 1964 a major submarine earthquake was followed by extensive flooding, as a result of which many of Niigata's larger buildings are conspicuously new.

The coastline on either side of the city — particularly north of Murakami and south, around Mount Yoneyama — is ruggedly attractive, though it shares the windswept bleakness for which the entire Japan Sea coast has a reputation. (The Japan Sea coast is sometimes referred to as Ura Nihon — the Back of Japan — because of its historical isolation from the main political and cultural centres.)

Niigata is the point of departure for the island of Sado, historically an island of exile and, like most of Japan's offshore islands, a place where rural life has been little affected by economic miracles. Sado remains virtually untouched by industry, though tourism has become vital enough for there to be no shortage of simple lodgings (minshuku) even in the smallest fishing villages.

Many of Sado's tourist destinations are linked to famous exiles. The Emperor Juntoku (1197-1242) spent 21 years on the island and is buried near the town of Mano. The militant Buddhist evangelist, Nichiren (1222-1282), lived for two years in a hut here, where he suffered from chronic diarrhoea. The hut is preserved as an object of pilgrimage.

But Sado was not always known for its gloom. Three hundred years ago the town of Aikawa had a population more than seven times larger than it has today on account of its thriving gold mine, now exhausted. The mine was worked by convict labour and a tiny section of its 250 miles (400 km) of underground tunnels is now open to visitors. The little museum at the mine provides an especially vivid impression of life in a 17th-century boom town.

Sado's main attraction is its unspoiled countryside and unhurried pace of life. An excellent way to see the island in panorama is to ascend Mount Donden by bus from Ryotsu. There is a government-run lodging house near the summit and the energetic visitor who stays overnight can descend to the opposite side of the island next day by means of a hiking course comprising the beds of old streams, open meadows and woodland paths. It takes about five hours.

Japan Alps

Nothing quite prepares the traveller for his or her first sight of the Japan Alps. They are the country's most wild and rugged mountains, as well as the most lofty, with peaks scraping the clouds at over 10,000 feet (3,000 metres).

The Japan Alps National Park is accessible from Matsumoto, a pleasant city on the eastern edge of the range and just a four-hour, limited-express train ride from Tokyo.

Matsumoto is famous for its six-storey castle, the moats and stone walls of which date from 1504, because it's the nation's only black castle. After climbing the steep steps to the top for a view out over the city and up to the high peaks, you can also see artifacts from the area in a small museum on the castle grounds.

Visitors with more time will want to wander north from the castle, about five minutes by foot, to Kaiichi Gakko, the oldest surviving school

Niigata in winter

from Japan's Meiji Era (1868-1912), a handsome building with Japanese-Victorian touches. It contains a small museum displaying educational materials from the period.

Matsumoto has a number of surviving storehouses with thick walls and black-tile roofs which dot the sidestreets between Matsumoto Station and the castle. Some have been put to modern use as shops or restaurants.

Kamikochi, just one and a half hours from Matsumoto by bus, or train and bus, should be the first stop in the national park. This is a base for mountain climbers, and there is accommodation of all kinds.

The narrow valley is surrounded entirely by steep mountains, the highest peaks snowcapped throughout much of the year. Winter snows close the area from late autumn to late spring. The trails on either side of the Azusa River, over which there are several swinging bridges, offer easy hiking for those wishing to have just a breath of the high-altitude air. For the more adventurous climber, there are numerous trails up into the mountains and on to the peaks from the valley in almost every direction.

Although surrounded by mountains, the Japanese never gave a thought to mountain hiking just for its own sake until an Englishman named Walter Weston explored the Japan Alps in the late 19th century. Today alpining is enjoying something of a boom among young people.

There are many hot spring resorts within a short drive of Kamikochi. Just one hour west through breathtaking scenery is Hirayu Onsen, an unspoiled mountain spa offering accommodation in traditional inns. All that intrudes here is towering Mount Norikura (9,928 feet or 3,026 metres high). From Hirayu it's just one hour by bus or car to Takayama on the western side of the range.

Takayama

This old town at the western foot of the Japan Alps, and just two and a half hours north of Nagoya by limited-express train, has managed to maintain its historic heritage in a way that few other Japanese towns have been able to.

There are modern reminders, for Takayama people do not want to live in a museum, but if the visitor concentrates on the sections between the Miya and Enoko rivers, and particularly in the small Sannomachi neighbourhood of shops with their wooden-slat exteriors and deep roof overhangs (to keep the deep snow off the front doorsteps), the visitor can't fail to be charmed.

Although a number of rich merchants' homes are open for visitors to see the interesting high-pitched roof timbers and small rear gardens, and there are many small museums displaying practically anything the town fathers haven't thrown away, not to mention the usual array of shrines and temples common to every Japanese town, it's the overall charm of Takayama, not its individual sights, that impresses the visitor.

An outdoor market where farmers come to sell their produce, fine woods from the surrounding rich timberlands, a park full of thatched-roof mountain dwellings brought down from the villages, lacquerware and ceramics, rustic inns serving wild roots and nuts from the Hida region and a number of antique shops filled with local folk art: all these combine to make Takayama the perfect place for quiet strolling in the mountain atmosphere unique to Japan.

The Region of Kyoto, Nara and Osaka (Kinki)

The region around Nara, Kyoto and Osaka is called Kinki or Kansai. These are two commonly used but overlapping terms. Kansai (West of the Barrier) is a large but not clearly defined cultural area. It is used in contrast to Kanto (East of the Barrier) which is the seven prefectures around Tokyo. Kinki (Near the Capital) is a more modern administrative term for the prefectures of Hyogo, Wakayama, Nara, Osaka, Kyoto, Shiga and Mie.

Kansai was the centre of the stage for nearly all the major developments in Japanese history and culture. The imperial court was in Kansai from the earliest days of the legendary Emperor Jimmu and only moved to Tokyo in 1868 at the time of the Meiji Restoration. Since that time the region has

THE REGION OF KYOTO, NARA AND OSAKA (KINKI)

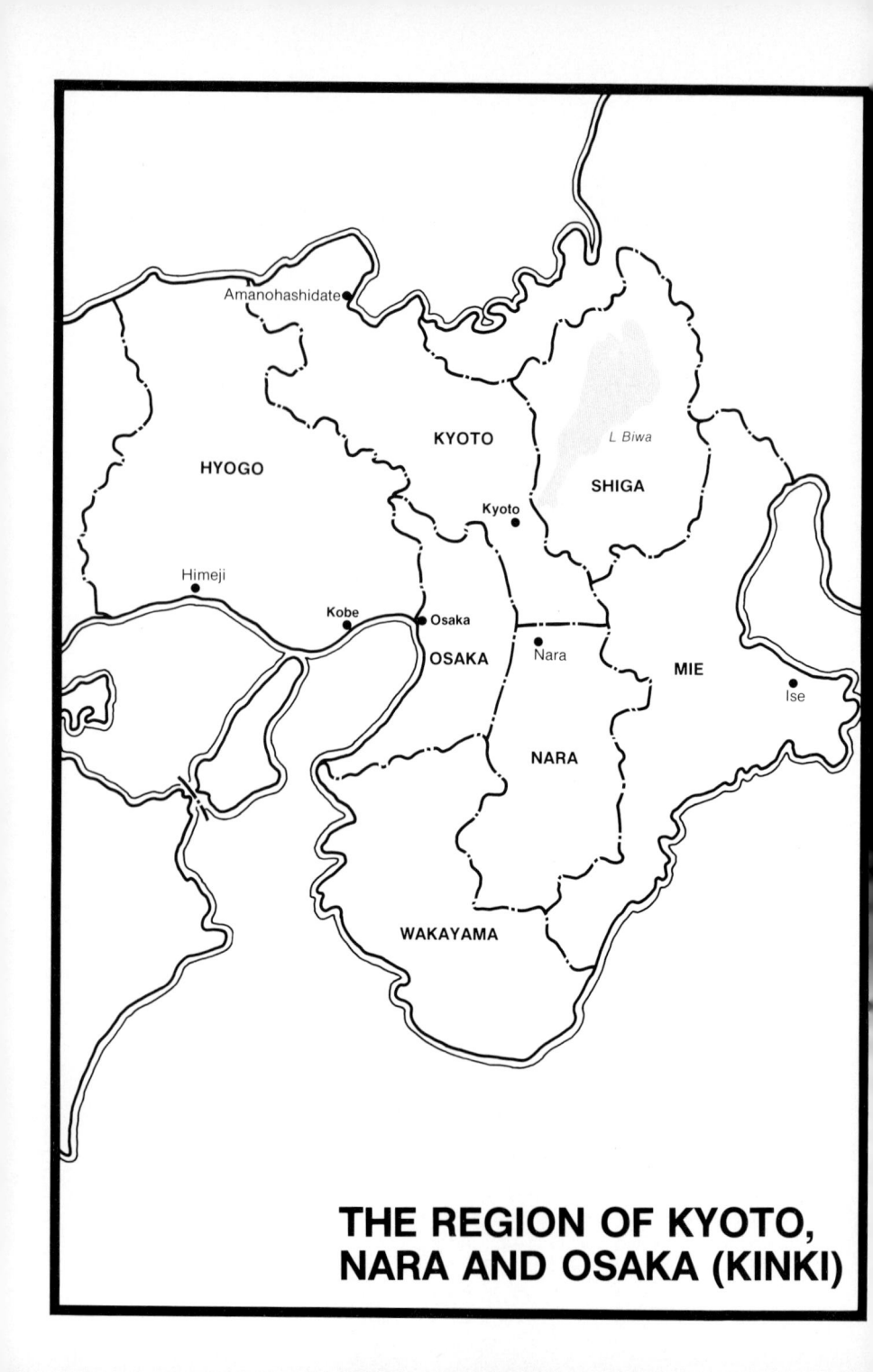

been in relative decline. Being dependent on material-oriented industries such as steel and textiles, it has suffered greatly from successive recessions. From a position of producing more than 35 percent of the nation's wealth it now contributes less than 20 percent. Business has tended to move to Tokyo.

Kansai, however, settled early because of the rice growing area of the Yamato plain and the relatively easy access to Korea and China, remains the richest cultural and historical area in Japan. Kansai people have their own dialect and a strong sense of their own identity. They, especially Kyoto people, regard themselves as by no means inferior to Tokyoites and look forward to a time when Kansai will regain its former pre-eminence.

Ise

Ise represents the beginning and the renewal of Shinto in Japan. It is the focus of the most sacred imperial rituals. The imperial family go there on important occasions; every Japanese prime minister travels the 400 miles (645 km) from Tokyo to pay an annual visit even though Shinto is no longer the official state religion. People go in their millions to this small, otherwise insignificant, town to visit the two most important shrines in the country. They go to pray to the gods; to purify themselves by washing in the Isuzu River; and to experience that sense of wonder before nature that is peculiarly Japanese.

The Inner Shrine, dedicated to Amaterasu, the Sun Goddess, houses the mirror which is one of the three imperial regalia. Legend has it that it was the mirror that enticed the Sun Goddess out of the darkness of her cave and so brought the sun into the world. This is the same sun that today you find on the Japanese flag, in the very name Nihon (Japan), and which ripens the rice in the fertile plains around Ise. The Outer Shrine, a few minutes on foot from Uji-Yamada station and 4 miles (6 km) from the Inner Shrine, contains articles dedicated to the Goddess of Agriculture, Toyouke.

Both shrines, set deep among beautiful cypress groves, enjoy the same status and relationship to the imperial household. They are completely rebuilt from the ground every twenty years. The next rebuilding (if the craftsmen can still be found) will be completed in 1993. It will be the 61st since records began in the 8th century. The shrines, constructed in the earliest Shimmei style, according to Shinto ritual are made only of natural materials. The wood, Japanese cypress, from the state forests at Kiso, is new and unpainted; the roofs are steep and thatched. No nails are used in the construction.

To get to the Inner Shrine visitors cross the bridge and wash their hands in the clear, flowing waters of the Isuzu River before treading the wide, grey pebbled path to the holy of holies. Cedar fences prevent visitors seeing anything but the outside of the shrine and they are expected to take off

Todaji (752), Nara

their hats and overcoats when near the shrine. It is, in fact, only since 1868 that Buddhist priests have been allowed to visit the two grand shrines.

Unless you go at the time of the important festivals in May, October and November you may find Ise, as a spectacle, anti-climactic; but as an experience to enable you to understand what makes the Japanese nation cohere, it is unsurpassed.

Nara

Nara is a civilised place where east meets east: attractive to resident and traveller alike. Its wooded countryside provides the backdrop for the oldest and finest art and architecture in Japan. A visit to Japan without seeing Nara is like going to Greece and not admiring the Parthenon. Nara is classical Japan.

The name Nara may refer to the city, ancient and modern, or a very large prefecture. The city, situated at the northern end of the prefecture, has a population of about 300,000. It is smaller today than in the 8th century when it was Japan's first permanent capital from 710-784.

Nara, the prefecture, includes the ancient Yamato plain and the surrounding mountains. Yamato is the old name for an area roughly equivalent to today's prefecture. The Yamato Plain is one of the very few extensive flat areas in Japan suitable for growing rice and it was this

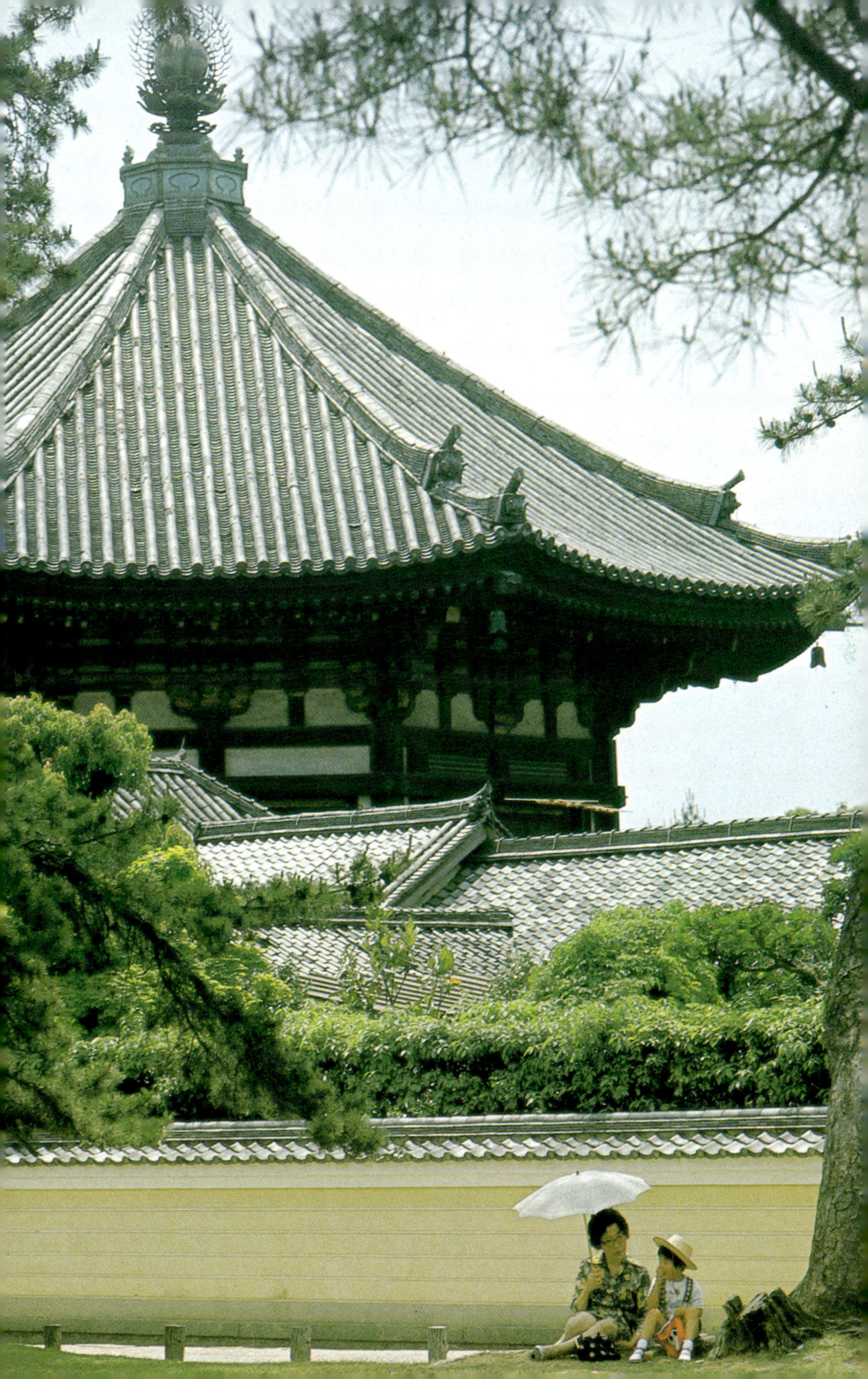

agricultural base which made the development of Nara, as the centre for the flowering of early Japanese civilisation, possible.

Lack of an early indigenous writing system (the Japanese had no writing system prior to the introduction of the Chinese script around the 4th century) and the fact that Japan is a country whose archaeological studies lag far behind its electronics, has meant that the details of early Japanese history are far from clear. However, it is known that by the 5th century, in the Yamato area, there existed a social system of clans. Each clan had a leader, and the emperor was at the head of the loosely knit, and often warring, assortment of patriarchal family units.

With an increasing population Yamato required a more sophisticated, higher level of social organisation and culture: these came from China through Korea, in the form of Confucianism and Buddhism. Around the year 552, in the reign of Emperor Kimmei (539-571), the first image of Buddha and some sutras came to Japan, along with strong recommendations for Japan to adopt the ways of continental China.

The first area to benefit from the influx of Chinese scholars and Korean craftsmen was Asuka, about 19 miles (30 km) south of Nara. The village of Asuka is in a country area (conveniently explored on a bicycle) dotted with temples, palace sites, burial mounds and carved granite figures. It was the reputed burial place of Jimmu Tenno, Japan's first emperor, and the centre of activity for the powerful Soga clan who accepted Buddhism to strengthen their hold on power. The oldest Buddhist image in Japan gleams in Asuka Temple. Nearby is Kashihara Archaeological Museum with its fine collection of artifacts from the Jomon and Asuka periods.

Between Asuka and Nara lies Horyuji, founded in 607 by the Regent Shotoku Taishi, an early supporter of Buddhism. It was a centre for cultural and academic activities. A close look at some of the statues reveals Persian and Cambodian influences. It has the oldest wooden pagoda in the world. In one corner of the very large complex of buildings is a monument to Langdon Warner, an American orientalist who was instrumental in saving Kyoto from bombing in the Second World War.

When the court moved north to Fujiwarakyo in 694 Prince Shiki wrote in the Manyoshu, a collection of poems from the period, as follows:
The gentle winds of Asuka
That fluttered the ladies' sleeves —
Now that the court is far removed,
Those breezes blow in vain.

Traditionally the court moved on the death of each emperor to escape from the associations of his death; but when the court moved to Nara in 710 it stayed, through a succession of emperors, for 74 years.

The modern city of Nara, 25 miles (40 km) from Kyoto and Osaka, is well governed. Highrise and basement development are against the law and only the noise of *pachinko* pinball parlours disturbs a quiet stroll down its back streets. But the glory of Nara is in its Deer Park and the ancient buildings all within comfortable walking distance of Nara Station.

The first building to catch the eye is the five-storey pagoda of Kofukuji, first built in 710. Most shrines and temples of any antiquity in Japan have been destroyed at least once in their lifetime, but usually rebuilt in the same style as the original. This makes for a discrepancy between the age of the materials and the style. The present Kofukuji pagoda is no exception and dates from 1426.

Situated in the large, wooded Deer Park is Kasuga Shrine with its 3,000 stone lanterns. The shrine is particularly beautiful in May with purple wistaria hanging over its vermilion-painted woodwork. As well as being one of the oldest and most venerated shrines in Japan it stands as a symbol of the Japanese ability to allow different religions to coexist. The same Japanese who worship the Shinto gods at Kasuga proceed on to Todaiji to pray to the Great Buddha, ten minutes away across the park.

Todaiji, with its great hall, probably the largest wooden building in the world, houses the largest bronze Buddha in the world. Built in 752 by Emperor Shomu it ranks with Chartres Cathedral as a massive monument to the labour of man in the service of religion. Nearby is the Shosoin. This is a wooden storehouse that contains the priceless possessions of the imperial court in use in the 8th century. It is opened to the public once a year for an airing in the presence of the Imperial Messenger.

Southeast from the gleaming gold rooftops of Todaiji and through the trees is the site of the ancient city of Nara. Called Heijokyo it was modelled on the Chinese city of Chang'an, the capital of the Tang Empire and probably the largest city in the world at the time.

Outside the Kintetsu Nara Station there is a modern bronze statue of Jian Zhen. He was a Chinese priest who tried to come to Japan five times in the 8th century, but each time failed, driven back by illness and rough seas. When he finally arrived on his sixth attempt he was blind. This did not prevent him from founding the Ritsu sect of Japanese Buddhism and the Toshodaiji, a temple six miles to the west of the city of Nara. He moved away from the city to escape the influence of large and powerful temples in Nara.

Nara is not only architecture; it is mountains, too. Mountains are sacred to the Japanese and the highest in Nara are in the south, rising to over 5,000 feet (1,500 metres). They include Odaigahara 5,561 feet (or 1,695 metres) above sea level, in the wettest part of Japan, and the Yoshino area. The Yoshino River is the most celebrated river in ancient books. Poets traditionally went to live there in isolation in the mountains. The poet Saigyo (1118-1190) had a hermitage there (it still exists) and Basho (1644-1694), the *haiku* poet, often praised its famous cherry blossoms and natural beauty. There is the tomb of Godaigo, the 14th century imperial

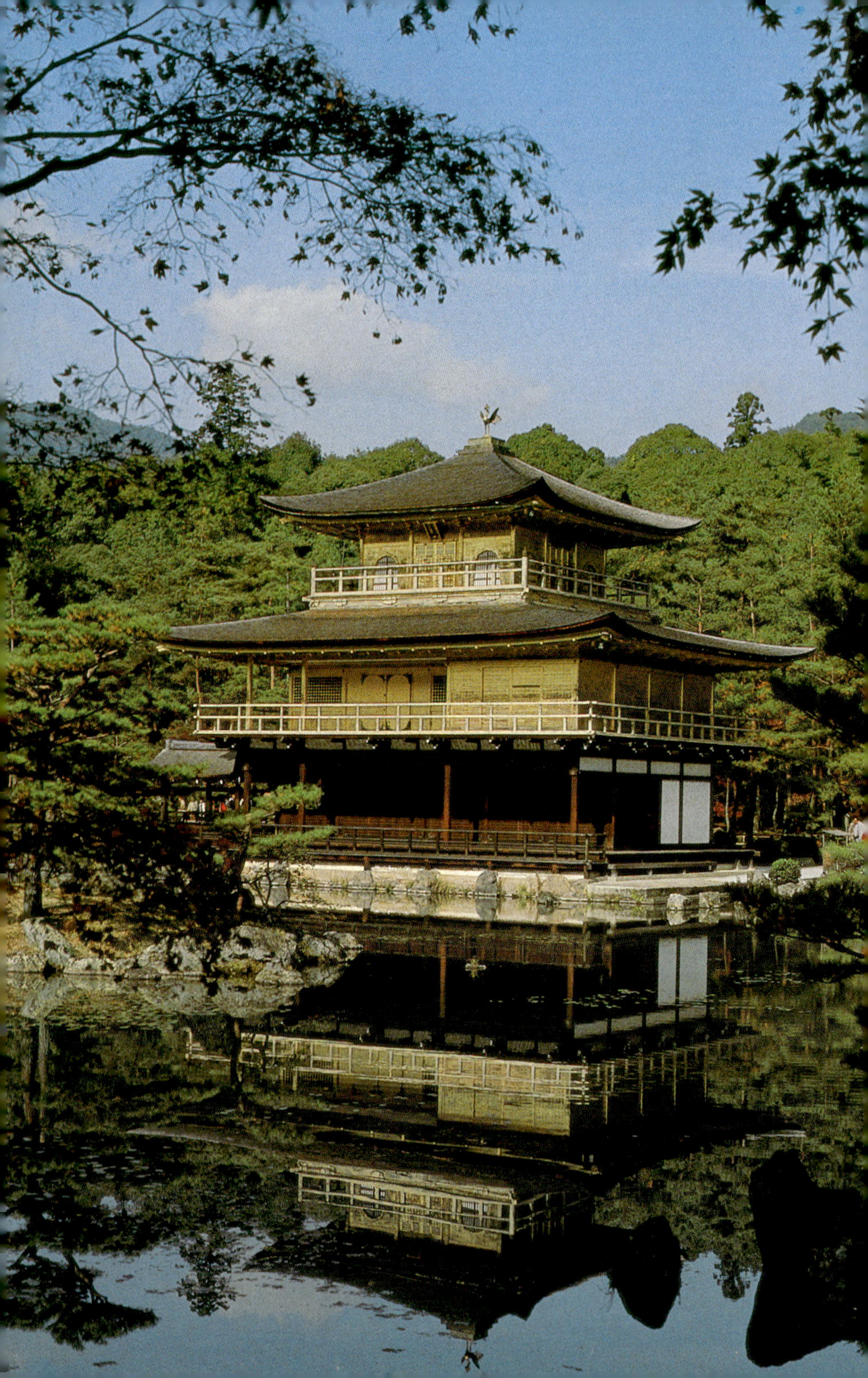

pretender, who set up his Southern Court in Yoshino in protest against the Kamakura Shogunate.

Festivals join the elements of folklore and religion to add drama to the gentle spirit of Nara. In January there is the grass burning on Wakakusa Hill, just north of Nara. March has the very ancient water drawing ceremony at Todaiji. In the autumn there is the ritual antler cutting at Kasuga Shrine, and in December near the winter solstice there is a 'festival of light' at the same shrine.

Kyoto

Kyoto is Japan's fifth largest city with a population of somewhat more than 1.5 million, and it holds a very special place in the hearts and minds of the Japanese people. The capital for more than a thousand years (794-1868), Kyoto has been the stage for much of the country's history. In addition, a great deal of what is considered Japanese culture had its beginning or reached its fullest development under the patronage of emperors, the nobility and the elite of the warrior class of Kyoto. Over the centuries the city has attracted and produced skilled artists and artisans whose abilities have been used in the service of the wealthy and the city's great Buddhist temples.

The site the Emperor Kammu chose for a new capital in 794 lies on the broad Yamashiro Plain which slopes gently to the south in the direction of Osaka. It is enclosed on its other three sides by a horseshoe of densely wooded, steep hills. The plain is watered by three major rivers, the Kamo, Katsura and Uji, which add to its natural beauty.

Mount Hiei, a conspicuous landmark, rises 2,684 feet (818 metres) in the northeast corner of the plain. It shields the city from the *kimon*, or 'unlucky quarter', the northeast being the direction from which evil and misfortune are believed most easily to enter a house or city. The halls of the Enryakuji, founded shortly after the city as the headquarters of the Tendai sect of Buddhism, dot its ridges and slopes. Splendid views of Kyoto, and to the east of the city of Otsu and Lake Biwa, can be had from several points on the mountain. Usually, some of Mount Hiei's band of indigenous monkeys can be seen along the roadside.

The highest peak in the semicircle of mountains is Atago, northwest of Kyoto, at 3,064 feet (934 metres). Atago Shrine on its summit is famous for giving protection against fire, an old problem in Kyoto, a city of one and two storey wooden buildings until this century. Atago also commands magnificent views of the city and the surrounding countryside.

Little remains of ancient Heiankyo (which is Kyoto's original name), but its street plan, a grid of intersecting avenues patterned after the old Chinese capital of Chang'an, has survived countless fires, wars, and renovations. This checkerboard layout makes it an easy city to get around in on foot, with Mount Hiei in the northeast and the north-south and east-west oriented main avenues.

Behind Kyoto's 20th century facade remains much of its past. The best of ten centuries of Japanese art and architecture can be seen in its formal buildings and villas and in its 1,658 temples and 406 Shinto shrines. Among the temples are the headquarters of 28 sects and subsects of Buddhism.

A focal point of Kyoto is the palace enclosure consisting of a park-like outer area (Gyoen), the Imperial Palace (Gosho) and the spacious stroll garden on the site of the Retired Emperor's Palace (Sento Gosho). The original palace was located farther west, but due to fires and political and economic problems this site, a secondary residence, has been used since the early 1300s. Its reconstructions (the last one was in 1885) have always been in the same form as the 10th century palace. Its all-wood construction, restrained decoration and austere ceremonial courtyard give it a serene timelessness.

Katsura, the occasional retreat of an imperial prince, and Shugakuin, which served the same purpose for Emperor Gomizuno-o, were built in the first part of the 17th century and mark high points in Japanese domestic and teahouse architecture as well as in garden design. The simple, clean lines of Katsura's living quarters have had great influence on 20th century western architecture.

The exquisite garden at Katsura presents a unified world in a small area. In contrast, Shugakuin is the epitome of the garden that 'borrows nature'. Its spectacular backdrop of Mount Hiei and panoramic view of Kyoto from above its wide Dragon Pond transcend all man-made boundaries.

The restrained design of the buildings of the palace and villas are excellent foils to the ornateness of Nijo Castle, built in the same period by the Tokugawa shoguns to show their domination over the emperor. Massive granite walls and moats conceal an elaborate garden with palm trees and large groupings of rare rocks. The residences are opulently decorated in gold and colour. Both the main garden and residences are excellent examples of the gorgeous art of the Momoyama Period.

Kyoto has also been a shogun's capital. The Ashikaga family, who held sway over the fortunes of Japan in the Muromachi Period (1392-1573), built an opulent palace that far outshone that of the emperor. Repeated battles took place within Kyoto between the middle 1400s and late 1500s, destroying most of the city's Muromachi splendour, but traces do remain in the elegant architecture and gardens of the Gold and Silver Pavilions, the remains of two magnificent retirement villas that were turned into temples after the deaths of the shoguns who built them.

The great Zen monasteries of Kenninji, Tofukuji, Nanzenji, Daitokuji, Myoshinji and Tenryuji (all founded in the 1200s and 1300s) offer a stark contrast to the Gold and Silver Pavilions. Massive wooden worship and teaching halls rise in severely landscaped grounds set with pines, stone walks and swept sand. The main buildings are surrounded by tiny sub-temples all but hidden behind thick earthen walls. These sub-temples were founded as residences for eminent Zen masters, as memorials to famous men, or as family temples for samurai and feudal lords. They contain jewel-like tea gardens that create a pocket of nature in the tiny space around diminutive teahouses. Side by side can be found meditation gardens composed of austere compositions of sand and stone, some with accents of moss and tiny plants as in the famous gardens at Ryoanji and the Daisenin in Daitokuji.

Traces of the sumptuous life-style of the Momoyama Period (1573-1603) which saw the lavish use of gold and Chinese motifs are found in the state apartments at Nishi Honganji, the head temple of the popular Shin sect of Buddhism. These imposing rooms are said to have been the audience chambers of the strongman-general Hideyoshi at his castle in Fushimi in the southeastern part of the city.

Gardens of the Momoyama Period combined every possible element, water, sand, rare rocks and unusual plants, in elaborate compositions. Fine examples remain at Nijo Castle, Nishi Honganji and at the Samboin, part of Daigoji. This last garden, begun under Hideyoshi from his own plans and completed thirty years after his death in 1598, is considered the exemplification of gardens of this time.

Daigoji, which spreads over an entire mountain in the southeast of the city, is a tumult of cherry blossoms in the spring and aglow with the fire of maple leaves in the autumn. Its red, five-storey pagoda (the oldest in Japan) and large halls stand majestically against a stunning backdrop of cedars, mountain and sky. This temple was, and is, a major teaching centre for the monastic Shingon sect. Until the end of the last century no woman was allowed in its upper precincts, an hour's climb up the mountainside.

The several sects of Buddhism founded in Kyoto have enjoyed centuries of patronage by the nobility, wealthy samurai and townsmen. Large and small Tendai, Shingon, Zen, Jodo and Shin temples contain matchless pieces of secular and religious art and architecture which are designated cultural properties by the central government. The nation's number one national treasure, a red pine statue of Miroku (Buddha of the Future) that has been sitting in serene contemplation since the early 600s is the pride of Koryuji, Kyoto's oldest temple, founded more than 150 years before the city.

Kyoto has exceptionally fine museums. The National Museum of Modern Art, the Kyoto City Museum and the Kyoto National Museum stage many exhibitions, major ones being held in the spring and autumn. The city's many private galleries and collections also provide superb displays of traditional and modern Japanese painting, calligraphy, ceramics, sculpture, lacquerware, and woven and dyed goods.

Rice planting festival, Hakone

Kyoto is a city of *matsuri*, festivals that range from small gatherings at neighbourhood shrines or temples to city-wide pageants. Each month has several. Many of these festivals are rooted in ancient beliefs and practices, such as in the comic religious plays (*kyogen*) given at Mibu and other temples and in the planting and harvesting festivals at the city's Shinto shrines.

The three biggest matsuri are the Aoi, or Hollyhock Festival in May, the Gion Festival in July and the Festival of the Ages in October. Aoi Matsuri originated in the Heian Period when yearly gifts were sent in state by the emperor to the gods of Kamigamo and Shimogamo, the tutelary shrines of Kyoto.

Gion Matsuri has its roots in a 9th century thanks offering to the god of Yasaka Shrine for ending a plague. Townsmen in what is now the financial and textile dealers' district made it into a yearly month-long series of events that has become Japan's most famous festival. Neighbourhood associations take charge of the putting together, manning and care of the heavy palanquins and gigantic, axleless carts that form the procession honouring the god of Yasaka on July 17th.

On the two nights preceding the 17th, Kyoto residents in colourful cotton summer kimonos and visitors to the city throng the participating neighbourhoods to admire family treasures displayed in the entrances of homes and businesses and to obtain close views of the exotic tapestries and mannequins in scenes from famous legends that decorate the floats. The

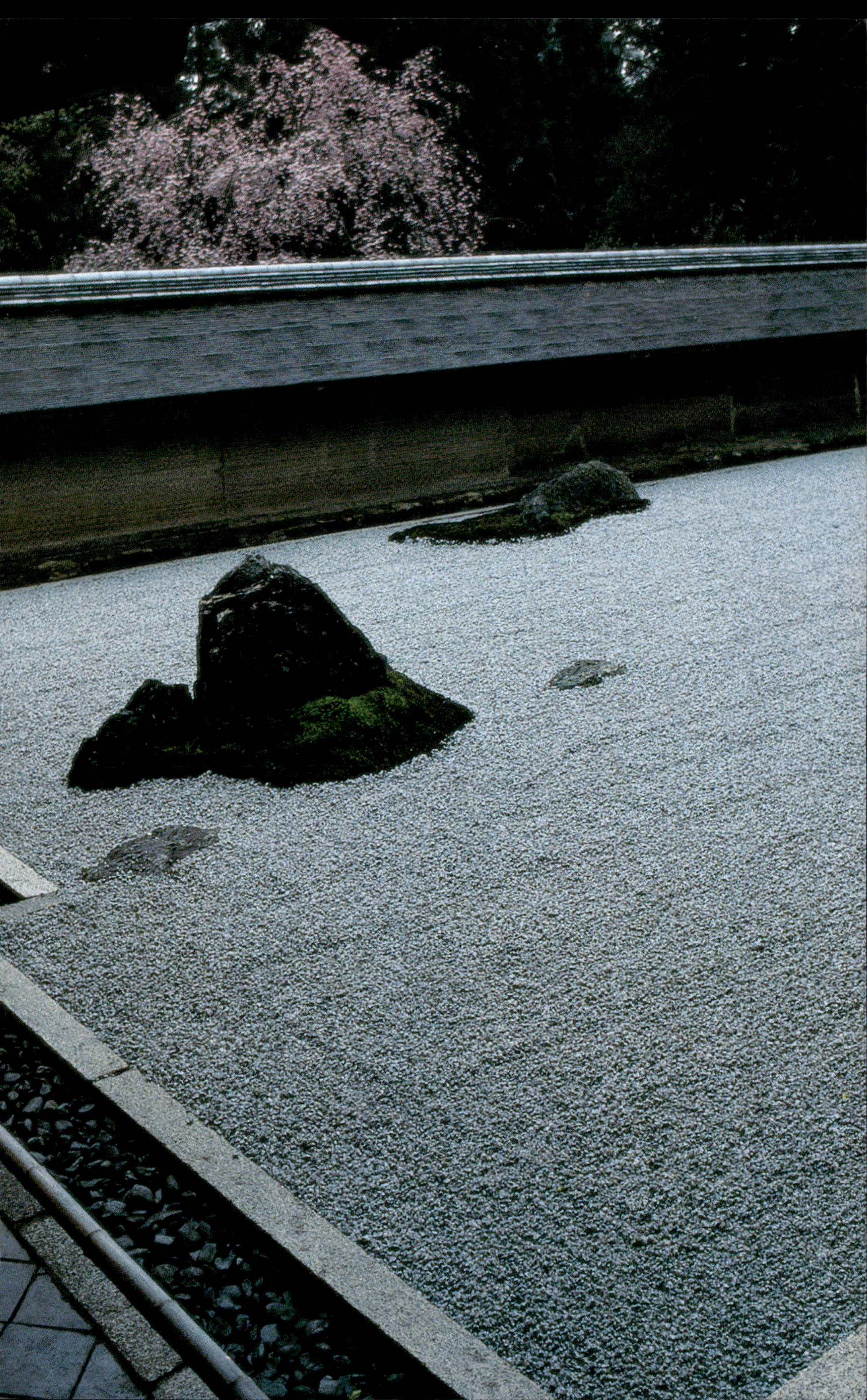

sounds of *Gion bayashi*, the festival's centuries-old music, the flutter of fans, tempting aromas from food stalls and the press of the crowd are an exciting part of this festival.

The Festival of the Ages, or Jidai Matsuri, is a product of this century that honours the emperors Kammu, founder of the city, and Komei, the last to reign entirely in Kyoto. Their deified spirits are ensconced in gilded palanquins at Heian Shrine and given an autumn outing accompanied by a long parade that portrays noted events in the city's past.

Kyoto means different things to different people. To some its essence is embodied in the splendour of its temples and treasures or in the atmosphere of a rural yesterday still found in the Saga and Ohara districts. But to many Kyoto's special ambience is present in the pottery district that surrounds Kiyomizudera (Japan's most visited temple) and in the walk from the Sannenzaka north along the eastern hills to Maruyama Park and Yasaka Shrine. Steep steps and cobbled streets lead past colourful shops and sober earthen walls that enclose temples, homes and elegant restaurants and inns set in beautiful gardens.

Kyoto has its neon and nightlife as well, but even that is touched by history. Just east of the main shopping streets the narrow alleys of Kiyamachi teem with bars, discos and eating places, but they gradually merge with one of Kyoto's several *geisha* quarters, Pontocho, on the banks of the Kamo River. Here, and in Gion across the bridge, evening brings glimpses of young geisha called *maiko* in colourful long-sleeved kimonos and trailing brocade *obi* wearing the swept-up hairstyle of the Edo Period (1603-1868) and of the older geisha in formal black kimonos with linings of scarlet and white as they hurry to parties at the quarter's teahouse-restaurants.

An hour or two of song, dance and chatter by these traditional entertainers who evolved from teahouse waitresses of the Kamakura Period is far too expensive for ordinary Japanese. The public can see them perform when the Pontocho and Gion associations stage their annual spring and autumn dances at theatres in both districts. Gion also has the Kabukiza, a traditional Japanese theatre in which *kabuki*, costume dramas and comic *manzai* and *rakugo* performances are held.

Osaka

Osaka, bombed flat in the Second World War, is the commercial, distributive and industrial heart of the Kansai area. It enjoys close ties with Chicago, a city it resembles. Osaka Bay is equivalent to Lake Michigan; rice replaces wheat as the main commodity on which commerce was founded.

Osaka is both city and prefecture and there is little but an administrative distinction between the two. The population of the city itself is 2.54 million, down from a 3.2 million high in 1940, a result of the war and the growth of outlying suburbs. The population of the Osaka metropolitan area, however, stands at 14 million and extends into Kobe to the west and Kyoto to the north. This means that 12 percent of the population of Japan lives in an area which is only one percent of Japan's total geographical area.

Osaka belies the literal translation of its modern name, 'big slope', as it developed on the flat area where the Yamato, Yodo and Muko rivers flow into Osaka Bay. Under its ancient name of Naniwa it was the site of an early capital in the 7th century. Being the port that commanded the east end of the Inland Sea, it was the nation's centre of trade and commerce.

One doesn't spend long in Osaka before learning the name Hideyoshi (1536-98). He made Osaka his military headquarters and in 1583 built the largest fortified castle in the country to consolidate his position as the major power in Japan. The impressive exterior of today's Osaka Castle has the same dimensions and style as the original; but apart from the enormous granite blocks of the walls and the wide moats, it dates from only 1931.

Hideyoshi's successor was Shogun Ieyasu. He initiated the caste system of samurai, farmer, craftsman, merchant, (*shi, no, ko, sho*) that placed merchants at the bottom of the social order and so fixed the character of Osaka. Like the Jews in Europe, the Osaka merchants had their activities limited, and were restricted in dress and possessions. In spite of the restrictions, or perhaps because of them, they amassed large fortunes. They lent money to the samurai, who needed to keep up appearances, and traded in rice, silk and other commodities. For some reason the government did not tax them directly and the merchants of Osaka became a *de facto* power. They laid the foundations for the large trading companies, like Mitsui and Mitsubishi, which dominate the Japanese financial world today. By the time of the Meiji Restoration in 1868 the merchants were rich and the samurai poor; but the moving of the emperor and his court to Tokyo started the decline of the power of Osaka compared to Tokyo.

To get an idea of how the merchants of old spent (and today's businessmen spend) their leisure and money, go at night to Dotombori, with its canal, near Namba. It is a riot of neon glitter and dazzle from the myriad signs of numerous small bars, cabarets, clubs and restaurants.

Osaka people are traditionally known for their love of food, as opposed to Kyoto people who prefer to spend their money on clothes, and Tokyoites who favour expensive footwear. In Dotombori, too, is the Asahiza, the theatre for *bunraku*.

Bunraku, strongly associated with Osaka since the late 17th century, takes it name from Uemura Bunrakken, a 19th-century puppeteer from nearby Awajishima. It is the most highly developed puppet theatre in the world and, like kabuki theatre, was the traditional entertainment of the middle and lower classes. (*No* theatre was for the court.) Chikamatsu, Japan's most gifted dramatist, wrote especially for the puppet theatre. The puppets themselves, over 3 feet (1 metre) high, are manipulated by men in

Osaka Castle (1586)

black, in full view of the audience. They are highly stylized and the lack of realism serves to intensify the emotional effect.

If Osaka doesn't have a large number of scenic spots it does have attractive seasonal events and festivals. From the 9th to the 11th of January each year is the Ebisu Festival. Ebisu, one of Seven Gods of Fortune, is the 'patron saint' of businessmen and merchants. Hundreds of thousands flock to the main Ebisu shrines to buy colourful talismans and to pray for good business in the coming year. On June 14th at Sumiyoshi Shrine, with its unique thatched buildings, is the traditional rice planting ceremony. Rice has a near religious significance for the Japanese and the ceremony with young girls planting rice in traditional costume to music is to ensure a good harvest. The Tenjin Matsuri (Water Festival), one of the three big name festivals in Japan, is held in floats on the river on July 24th and 25th. Osaka was known as the Water Capital and had 808 bridges over its canals and rivers in the Tokugawa Period. Today there are 1,500 bridges for road and rail connections.

Kobe

Kobe was officially opened as a port to foreign trade in 1868, one of six concession areas allotted for some three decades to foreigners. It has grown from a sparsely-populated sandy stretch of beach to a city of nearly 1.4

書画　骨董　書画
風雅堂

million people, with one of the largest and most modern ports in the world.

The business centre is the Sannomiya area, also the starting point of a mile-long shopping street. Japan's first fully-computerized driverless train runs the short distance from Sannomiya to Port Island, an island of reclaimed land taken from the hills west of Kobe.

The forested Rokko mountain range (highest point 3,057 feet or 932 metres) forms a green backdrop to the city. Cableways carry passengers to the top where there's an artificial skiing ground, a farm popular with city children, an alpine garden, and a view of the night lights below. On the other side of the mountains is sleepy Arima, one of Japan's oldest hot spring resorts.

At the foot of Mount Rokko lies the Nada district, traditionally acclaimed for its excellent sake. Modern breweries sit side by side with 150-year-old sake cellars, one of which is now an interesting museum.

In the hilly Kitanocho section, foreign traders of the Meiji (1868-1912) and Taisho (1912-26) eras built homes in the European style of the day. As late as 1955 two hundred of these houses remained, but increasing urban development has reduced the number to about 30 today. A recent television serial about a Japanese woman who married a German baker in Kitanocho has sparked a sightseeing boom among young Japanese who come looking for a touch of Western exotica. Several of the old foreign houses have been restored and are open to the public.

Himeji

There are castles all over Japan, a common focal point in practically every city. But architectural critics give highest praise to Himeji Castle, whose five-storey white donjon rises north from Himeji Station, just an hour by 'Bullet Train' west of Kyoto.

The castles were first built by local feudal lords for defence, but during the long and peaceful Edo Period (1603-1868), they served primarily as symbols of a local lord's authority over his fief. Although the multi-storeyed towers are their most dramatic feature, these were lookouts, not living quarters, and Hiemji Castle is the only one extant with all its outbuildings for the lord and his retinue.

The Japanese call Himeji the Egret Castle because from a distance it looks like a white bird sweeping over the rice fields. It is quite possible to wander for a couple of hours through the maze of corridors and walkways of the 78 separate buildings where comfort seemed to be an afterthought compared with worrying about the enemy.

Amanohashidate

Amanohashidate (Floating Bridge of Heaven) is a sandbar, 2.24 miles (3.6 km) long, which stretches across the Bay of Miyazu on the Japan Sea coast, enclosing half of the bay like a lagoon. The bar is covered with pine trees, the number of which grows year by year, and, like Matsushima and Miyajima, it is nationally famous as one of the 'three most beautiful views' in Japan.

There are three ways a visitor can enjoy it. He can walk along it (a short bridge connects the southern end to the mainland) though the view across the bay that this stroll affords is somewhat spoiled by the tourist hotels. He can take a sight seeing boat along either side of it, which provides a more comprehensive view, or he can do what visitors are traditionally advised to do: climb (or take the cable car) up to Kasamatsu Park on the northern side of the bay, stand on a stone bench there with his back to the sandbar, bend down and look at it through his legs. This is said to give him the impression that the 'Floating Bridge' is actually floating, though it is worth wondering who first made that discovery.

Western Honshu (Chugoku)

The western end of Honshu (Chugoku, or Middle Country) is geographically a microcosm of the whole island. One side (the southern side) is densely populated and very developed industrially, to the extent that the once-romantic Inland Sea which it borders has been badly affected by industrial pollution. The Japan Sea coast side, however, remaining comparatively unspoiled, is far more relaxed in atmosphere, and the San-In Kaigan National Park, which is its main attraction, can justly claim to include some of the most beautiful coastline in the country. Inland, the area is very mountainous and almost all of the large cities are on the coasts.

Tourists who venture this far west are often on their way to Kyushu and, because they tend to pass through it rather than explore it, the Chugoku region as a whole has suffered less from commercial tourist developments than some other areas of Japan.

Okayama City and Kurashiki

Okayama Prefecture is the modern name for the area once known as the Kibi kingdom. In the early centuries of our era a great culture flourished on the Kibi plains, the remains of which are still to be seen though its history is still shrouded in mystery. Huge tumuli, the remains of an ancient fortress probably bigger than Windsor Castle in England, foundations of various buildings and the ruins of ancient villages can be seen in the delightful countryside between Okayama City and Kurashiki City.

Kibitsu Shrine was built between 1392 and 1427. Situated on the side of Mount Naka 5 miles (8.4 km) from Okayama City, it commemorates the spirit of Prince Kibitsuhiko no Mikoto who was ordered to Kibi by the 5th

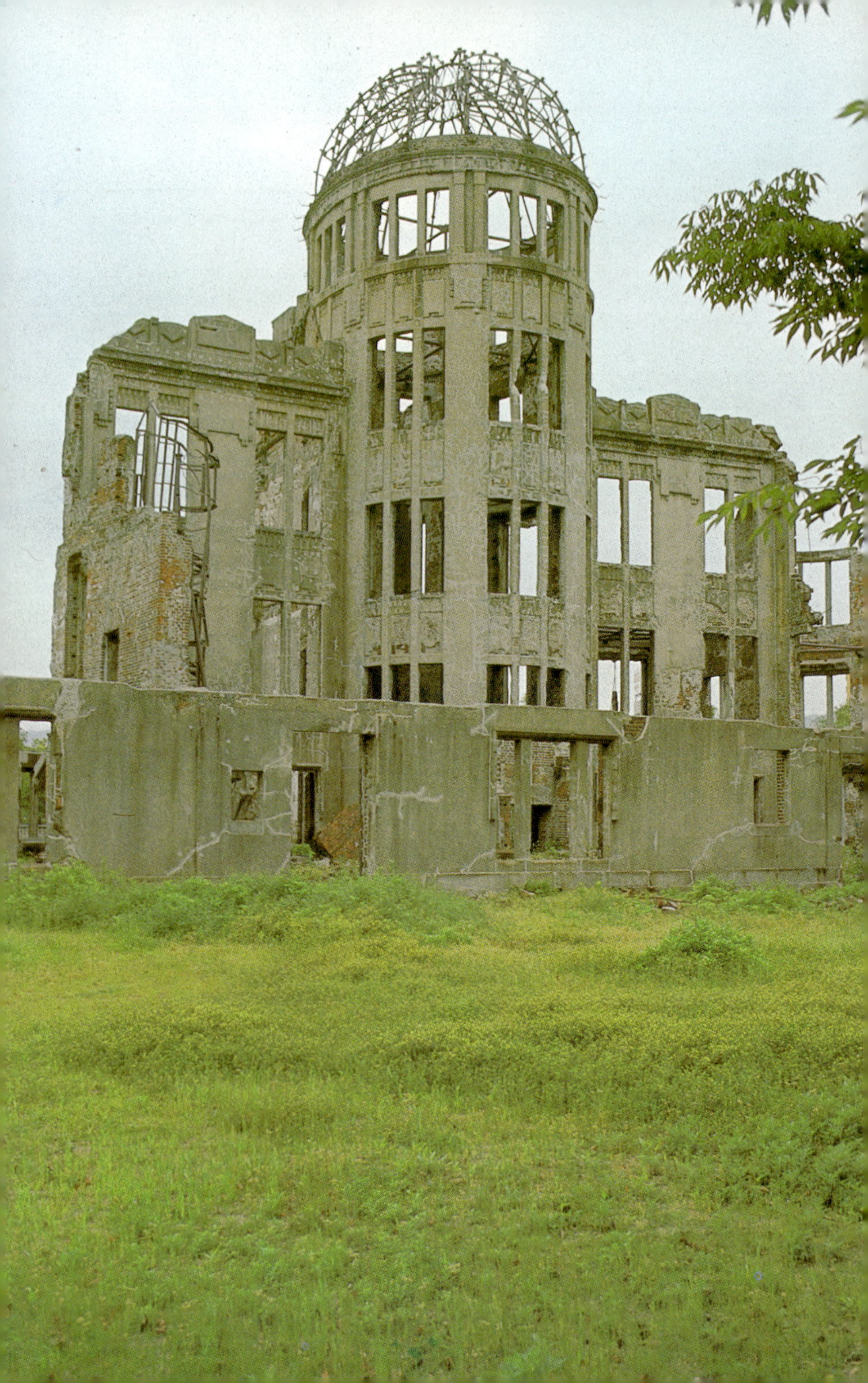

Ruined dome over which the Hiroshima bomb exploded, 8:15am August 6, 1945

century Emperor Ojin to suppress a local uprising. The style of the building is unique and the main shrine is set on a brilliant white base to give the impression that it rests on a shimmering sea. A very long, beautiful, roof-tiled passageway leads down the side of the hill to the ancient shrine barracks and is lined on each side by smaller shrines and an impressive archery pavilion.

Komorizuka Tomb in the same area is believed in local folklore to be the burial place of the Black Princess who was the concubine of the 6th century Emperor Nintoku. It is a fine example of a keyhole shaped tumulus, and the stone burial vault, in which lies a huge stone coffin, can easily be entered. The stone coffin weighing about 5 tons has recently been proven to have come from far-off Hyogo Prefecture.

The Kura in Kurashiki means a warehouse, and along the willow-lined canal of the city can be found carefully-restored 17th and 18th century white-walled and black-tiled storehouses set in the grounds of the homes of the merchants. These buildings are national treasures, almost the only examples of an 18th century merchant community's left in Japan. Today through the patronage of the Ohara family these buildings house museums. The Ohara Museum of Art has one of the finest collections of French Impressionists in Asia. The nearby Ceramic Gallery contains the works of Hamada, Leach, Kawai and Tomimoto. There is also the Oriental Gallery set in the same grounds. The Archaeological Museum contains a fine collection of artifacts from the ancient Kibi kingdom. The Mingeikan (Folk Museum) is well worth a visit. It boasts a brilliant collection of Japanese and international folk art.

Okayama City, the prefectural capital city, was badly damaged during World War II, but still contains the Korakuen, one of the three most famous gardens in Japan and part of the castle grounds of the feudal lord Ikeda. It was designed by a famous 18th century landscape gardener.

Hiroshima and Miyajima

No visitor to Hiroshima can fail to associate the city with the dropping of the atomic bomb there on August 6th, 1945. Rebuilt from the rubble, Hiroshima is once again the principal administrative and commercial centre of the Chugoku region. It is a city of spacious roads, busy nightlife areas, modern shopping arcades, the home of a popular baseball club, and possesses a general sense of vitality and well-being. Nevertheless, the chief centres of tourist interest (one can hardly call them attractions) are those that recall the atomic tragedy and which the residents regard both as memorials to human folly and as prayers for peace.

The symbol of the city is the 'Dome', situated at the northeast corner of the Peace Memorial Park. It tops the old Industry Promotion Building which has been left in its gutted state as a reminder of Hiroshima's suffering. It was

WESTERN HONSHU (CHUGOKU)

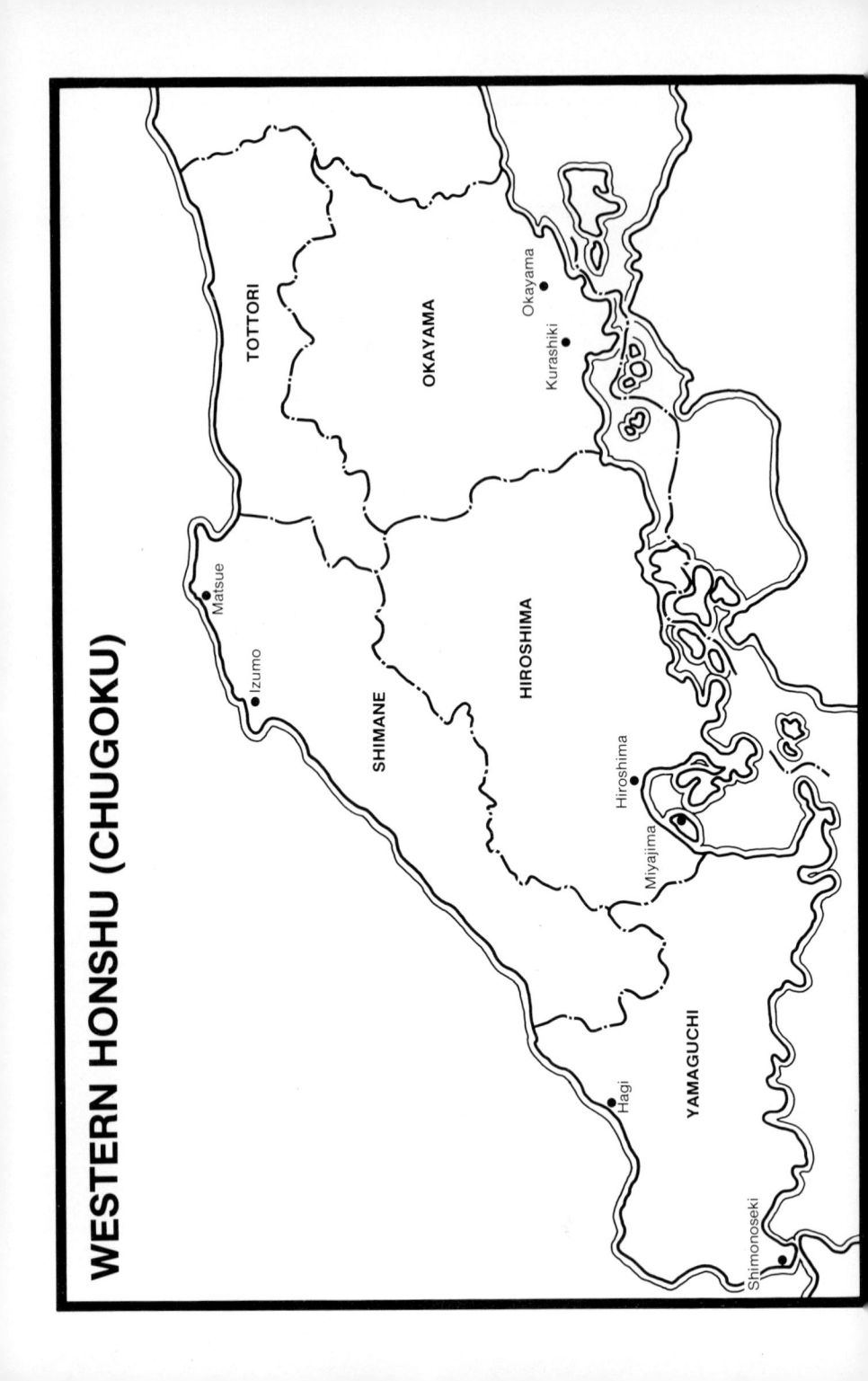

above this building that the bomb exploded.

On the other side of the park stands the Peace Memorial Museum which contains exhibits related to the bombing. The most harrowing of these are the photographs, but there are also artifacts that convey the nature of the damage, and there is a horrific display of waxwork figures representing victims of the bomb.

The park has a number of monuments, the most eloquent of which is the stone chest containing the names of the dead. It is inscribed, 'Sleep in peace. The mistake will not be repeated.' Each year, on the anniversary of the bombing, large numbers of people gather here to remember the victims and to issue calls for nuclear disarmament.

Some 12 miles (20 km) west of Hiroshima lies the island of Miyajima which, together with its famous shrine, is considered one of the 'three most beautiful sights' in Japan. The shrine's principal buildings and corridors are built on piles over the sea so that, at high tide, the whole complex appears to float. This is also true of the great red *torii* gate - the largest in Japan — which stands well out into the sea itself and is undoubtedly the most photographed of all Shinto edifices.

Hagi

The city of Hagi is chiefly famous for its 400-year-old pottery industry, whose speciality is the highly-prized ceremonial tea bowls which were copied long ago from Korean models. (Many of Japan's pioneer potters were either Korean themselves or had Korean teachers.) Though the city's castle has vanished (except for the ruined foundations, now part of a park), Hagi is renowned for that old world charm which seems to survive only in castle towns. This charm has not entirely given way before the modernization of the port and fisheries.

Hagi is a good base from which to explore the surrounding coastline, remarkable for its picturesque bays and for its many small offshore islands, reminiscent of the Inland Sea, but quieter and less spoiled. The largest, Omi Island near Nagato, is connected to the mainland by a bridge and has a serene, relaxing landscape, in contrast to the more rugged scenery that characterizes the Japan Sea coast as a whole.

Matsue and Izumo

The city of Matsue is dominated by one of the few surviving Japanese castles not reconstructed in modern times. Restorations have been made, but the present donjon dates from 1642 and provides a fine example of the elegance of castle architecture, as well as an excellent view over the city and surrounding countryside.

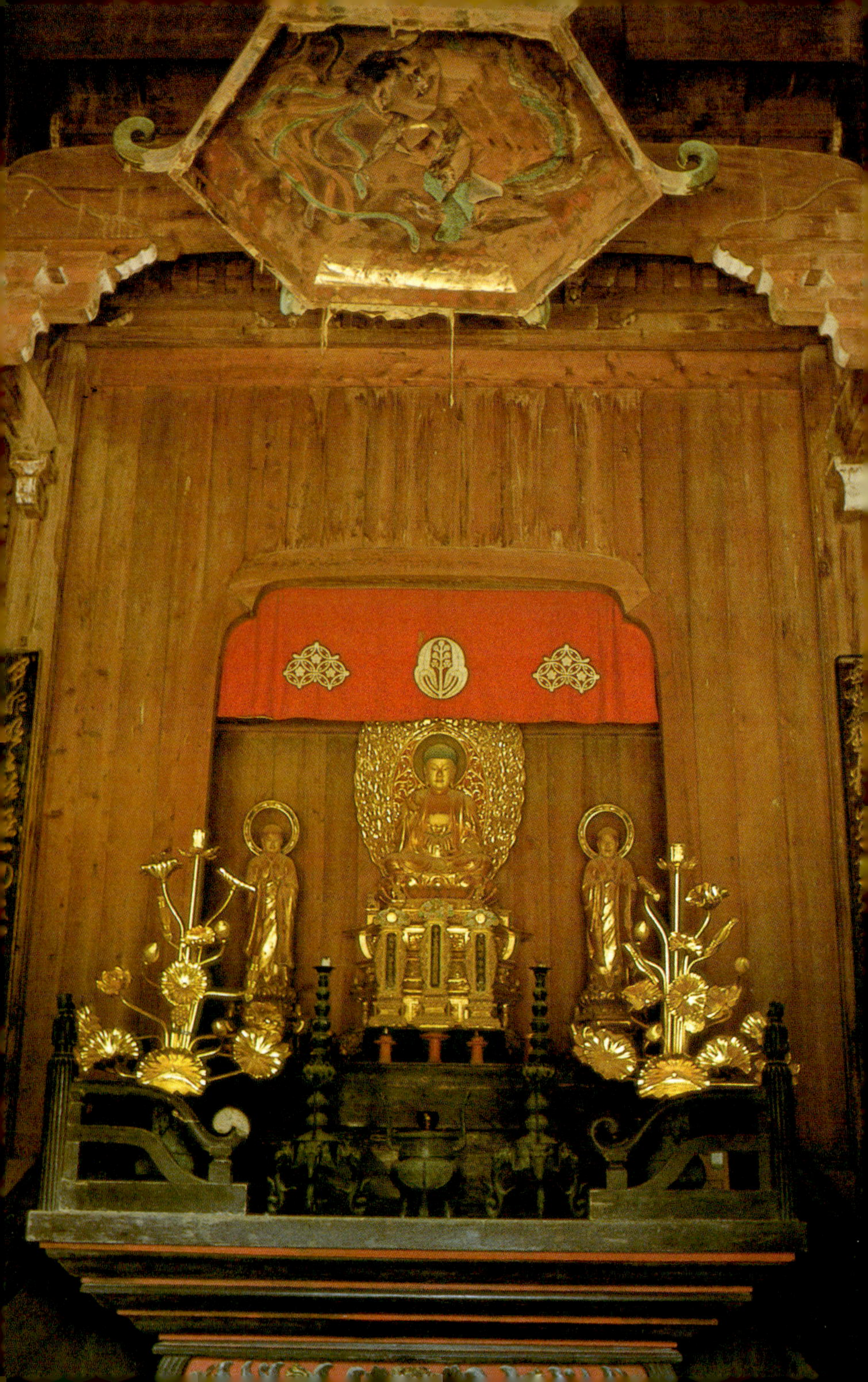

Sanno Matsuri, Tokyo

Many Japanese visitors associate Matsue primarily with the expatriate author and teacher, Lafcadio Hearn (1850-1904). This is ironical since, out of 16 years in Japan, Hearn spent only 7 months in Matsue. But the city provided him with his first glimpse of 'the interior' (he had previously worked as a reporter in cosmopolitan Yokohama) and it was here that he married and took Japanese nationality, adopting the name Koizumi Yakumo. His house, though still a private residence, is open to visitors and there is a small museum of his life and work next door. Matsue has made much of its association with Hearn, whose name, little known abroad, is a household word in Japan. The city boasts several bars, two coffee shops, a pet shop and a beauty parlour named after him.

Some 25 miles (40 km) west of Matsue stands the great Shinto shrine of Izumo Taisha — the oldest shrine in the country and, after Ise, the most revered. Like much else that is 'old' in Japan, the shrine complex has been rebuilt in comparatively recent times (1874), but the style of architecture (particularly the steeply sloping thatched roofs with their striking crossbeams) is among the most ancient in Japan. Hearn's diary contains an account of his emotions upon standing before the Izumo shrine: 'This is the Shrine of the Father of a Race; this is the symbolic centre of a nation's reverence for its past.' It is difficult to visit Izumo without succumbing to a similar sense of awe. So revered is the shrine that many hundreds of gods from all over the country are said to congregate here for a conference each October; which has resulted in October being known throughout the rest of Japan as *Kannazuki* (the Month of No Gods).

The Island of Shikoku

Although it is Japan's fourth island in size, the foreign visitor seldom hears much about Shikoku, and for those with a penchant for the unknown, that's reason enough to make the short trip across the Inland Sea from the main island of Honshu.

The island is divided into four (*shi*) distinct regions (*koku*), today's four prefectures corresponding with the former four feudal fiefs. Among the four major cities of Takamatsu, Matsuyama, Kochi and Tokushima, Takamatsu is the most easily accessible from Honshu, and probably the most interesting for the foreigner.

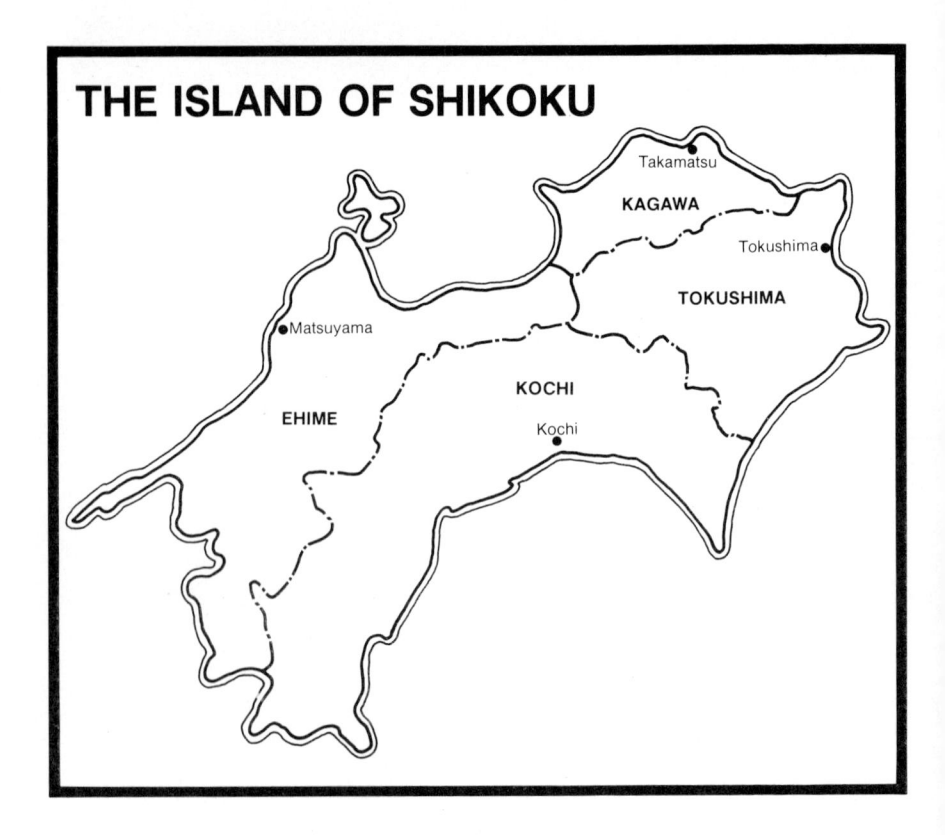

THE ISLAND OF SHIKOKU

- Takamatsu
- KAGAWA
- Tokushima
- TOKUSHIMA
- Matsuyama
- KOCHI
- EHIME
- Kochi

Takamatsu

Although Japan has many port cities, there are few in which the visitor is really aware of the harbour. Not so in Takamatsu, Shikoku's chief city, where the business district sits right on the waterfront. By Japan National Railways ferry it's just a one hour trip across the Inland Sea to Uno on Honshu.

The city's chief attraction is Ritsurin Park, one of the most attractive stroll gardens in Japan. This was once the garden of a villa owned by the Matsudaira family who did much to shape the island's history. The designer took full advantage of the natural site below a well-forested hill. Features include a series of ponds connected by bridges. Ritsurin is part of a city park including a zoo, folk art gallery and government museum.

Near Takamatsu Pier is the site of a castle with only its turrets and one gate remaining. The high hill to the east, once an island, is known as Yashima and is interesting to the Japanese because it was the site of a famous battle late in the 12th century between the Taira and Minamoto clans which tipped the power scales in favour of the Minamoto family and put the nation under military authority that essentially lasted until the mid-19th century.

Tokushima

A sleepy prefectural capital most of the year, Tokushima citizens take to the streets en masse from August 15th to 18th to dance their *awa dori* to the accompaniment of the Japanese *shamisen* (a traditional stringed instrument), flutes and drums.

Just east of the station, Tokushima Park covers a thickly wooded hill where a feudal lord's castle once sat. A fine garden remains, and there is also a zoo and recreational facilities.

Southwest of the station, Bizan Park draws visitors during the cherry blossom season, and any time of the year for distant views of the Inland Sea.

Tokushima is a convenient point from which to travel to Naruto for a boat trip to view the whirlpools formed by water rushing through the narrow channel of the Naruto Straits between Shikoku and Awaji Island.

Kochi

Kochi has a castle dating from 1748, which is still standing and its five-storey donjon is visible from many areas of this small city.

Kochi is the gateway to Ashizuri Cape, a subtropical peninsula covered with small palms and banyan trees. The cape can be reached by three different routes, but Ashizuri Skyline toll highway perhaps offers the most spectacular sea and mountain views, reminiscent of California's Big Sur coastline.

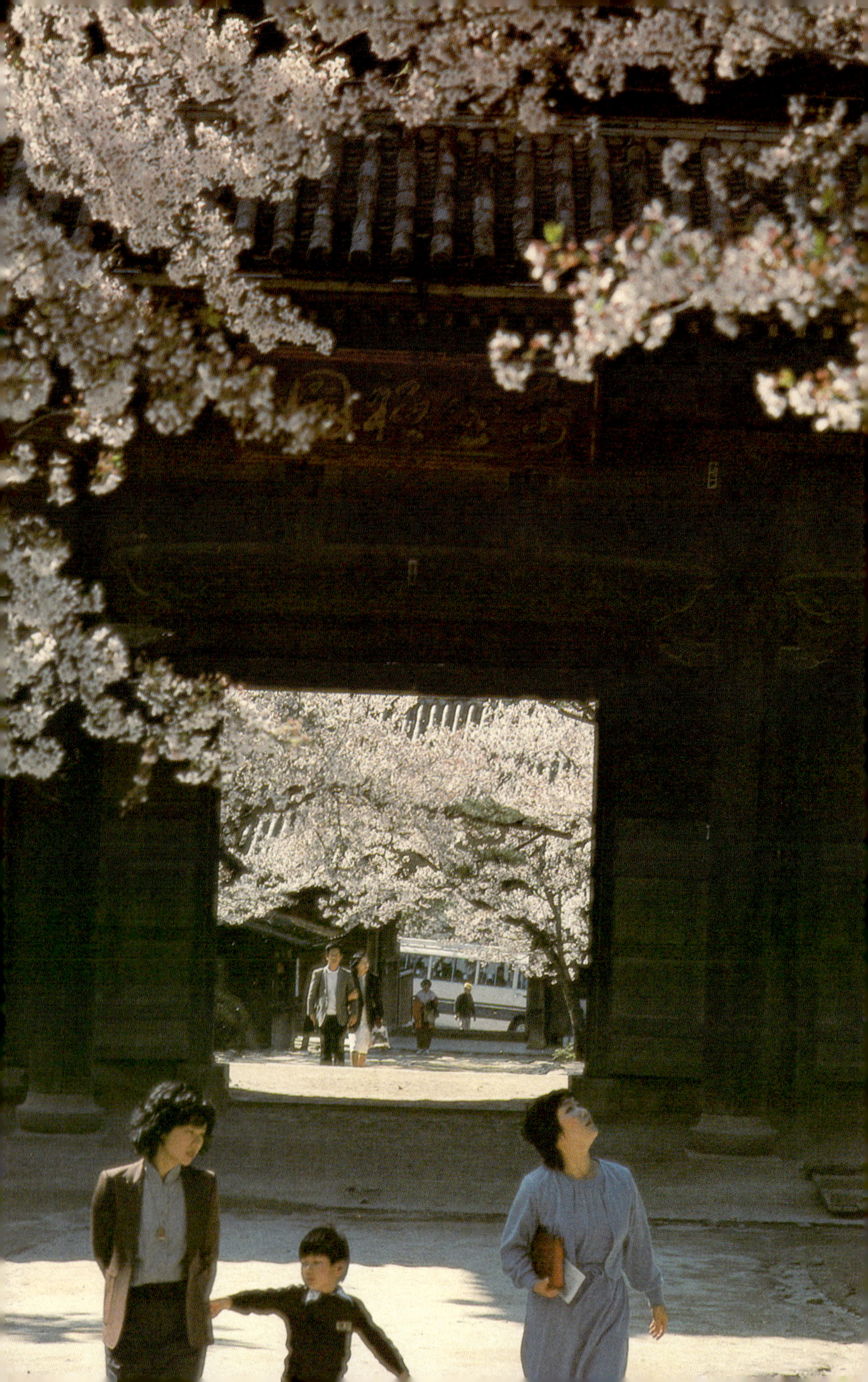

North of Ashizuri is Uwajima, where a Japanese version of a bullfight is held approximately once each month. No humans are involved here, just two bulls locking horns in a test of strength.

Matsuyama

Matsuyama Castle with its three-storey tower is one of Japan's best preserved. It is easily accessible by ropeway from the east side of Matsuyama Park, a hill perched prominently in the centre of town. It dates from 1602. The approach is by four gates and enclosures. Much of the space inside is used to exhibit feudal palanquins, armour and swords, all belonging to the Matsudaira family of Takamatsu.

Besides the castle, Matsuyama's other big draw is Dogo Onsen, a spa which is actually part of the city proper. Unlike many spas, this one has a public bath house of extraordinary proportions, and has been frequented by many of Japan's celebrities. The imperial family visited it in 1899 and had a bath house of their very own carved out of stone.

Soseki Natsume, Japan's famous Meiji era writer, taught at a Matsuyama school for a brief period, and his antics with the bumbling school administrators are the subject of his humorous novel *Botchan*.

The Island of Kyushu

Historically, the island of Kyushu has been the chief gateway through which continental and other foreign influences made their way into Japan. Historians are not fully agreed on where the Japanese race originated, but the earliest settlements were certainly in northern Kyushu, suggesting that the settlers may have come via Korea. When Christianity was introduced in the mid-16th century Kyushu became its stronghold, and even during the two centuries when Japan was deliberately closed to the rest of the world there was a small foreign trading post in Kyushu through which firearms and medicines, among other things, were imported.

Kyushu is rich in scenic beauty as well as in history. The highest peaks are volcanic, including the still-active Mounts Aso, Kirishima and Sakurajima, and the areas around these, now national parks, offer countryside as attractive as any in Japan. Northern Kyushu (especially the cities of Kitakyushu and Fukuoka) is heavily industrialized, having been the centre of Japan's now depleted coal industry, while the south is almost entirely rural, quiet, rugged, and comparatively sparsely populated.

Nagasaki

Like Hiroshima, the city of Nagasaki was largely destroyed by an atomic bomb in August 1945 and, as at Hiroshima, this tragedy has been

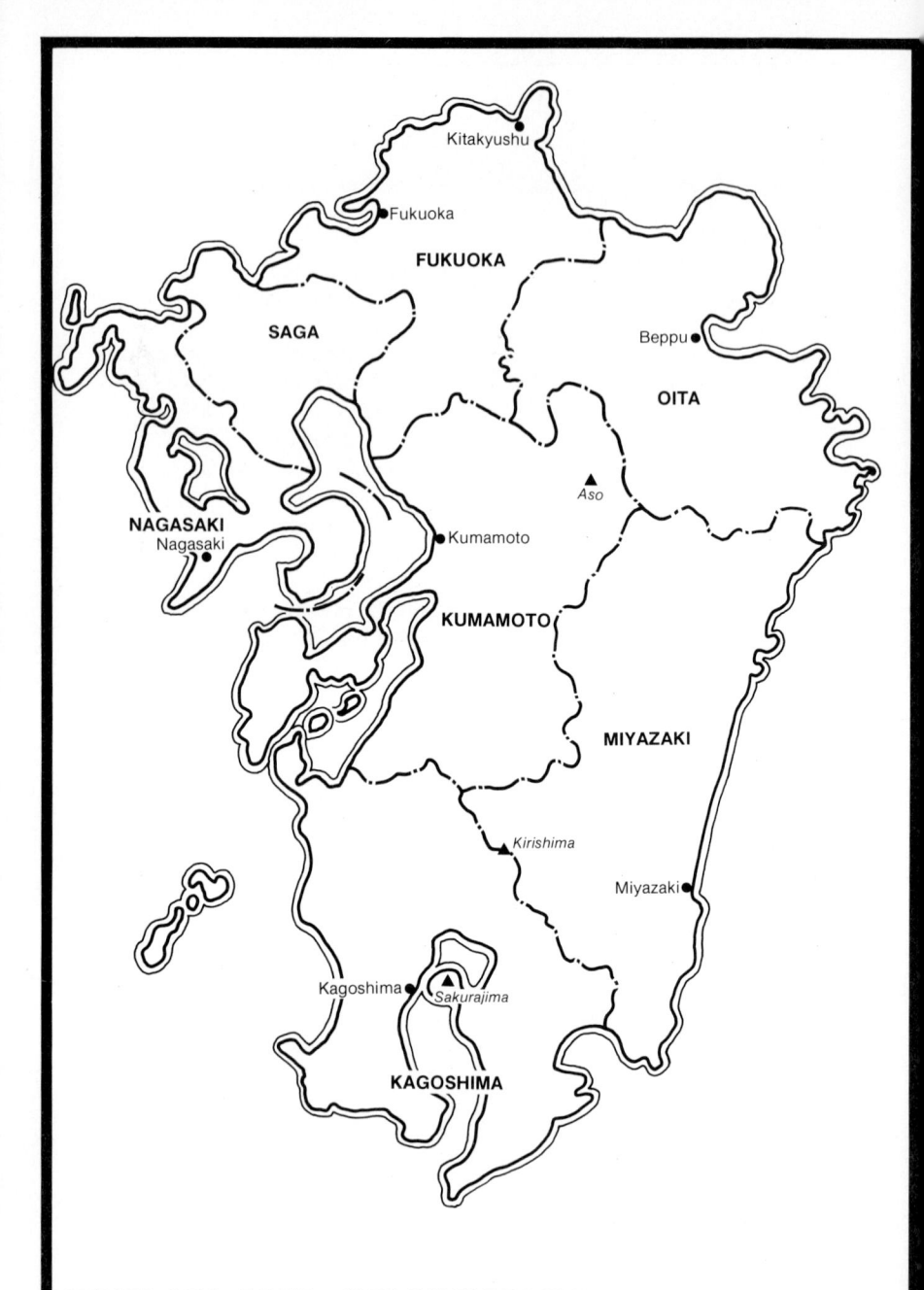

THE ISLAND OF KYUSHU

commemorated by the building of a Peace Park. However, the visitor to Nagasaki is less likely to focus his attention there than on the reconstructed city itself, with its long, well-sheltered bay, its attractive sloping streets and terraces, and its many earlier historical associations, particularly with Christianity.

Less than 50 years after its introduction to Japan, Christianity was outlawed, and on February 5th, 1597, twenty Japanese Christians and six foreign priests were crucified at Nagasaki (crucifixion being the normal form of execution for commoners throughout the feudal period). Miracles are said to have followed the deaths of these martyrs and today a monument commemorates them.

Persecution of Christians continued until the opening of Japan to foreign trade in 1854. When Oura Catholic Church was established in Nagasaki in 1865, it quickly became clear that the city and surrounding countryside had harboured thousands of secret Christians throughout the closed centuries, when groups of loyal adherents to the religion revealed themselves. The church survived the atomic bombing and remains the oldest Gothic style building in Japan.

In 1639, partly as a result of the defiant proselytizing activity of Portuguese priests, all foreigners were summarily expelled from Japan, except for a small community of Dutch (and some Chinese) traders, who were allowed to occupy the tiny man-made island of Deshima in Nagasaki Bay. Here they remained during the 215 years of isolation, the sole agents for the introduction of foreign ideas and artifacts into Japan. They succeeded so well in this that, when the country reopened, students flocked from all over Japan to Nagasaki, which they regarded as a major centre of Western learning. Deshima Island has been almost entirely obliterated by the construction of harbour facilities and Japan's largest shipyard.

Nagasaki is also famous as the setting for Puccini's opera *Madame Butterfly*, and one fine old foreign mansion, Glover House, is sometimes pointed out to credulous visitors as the place where Chocho-san (Madame Butterfly) lived.

The Shimabara Peninsula, southeast of Nagasaki, is famous as the site of a Christian uprising in 1637-1638, which was suppressed with such brutality that over 30,000 rebels were massacred. The Goto Islands, which lie due west of Nagasaki, were also a stronghold of secret Christianity. Today they offer the visitor not pressed for time a peaceful glimpse of southern Japan at its most rural and untroubled.

Kumamoto and Mount Aso

Kumamoto is a large modern commercial city, and thus an uncharacteristic capital for a prefecture which contains some of the most

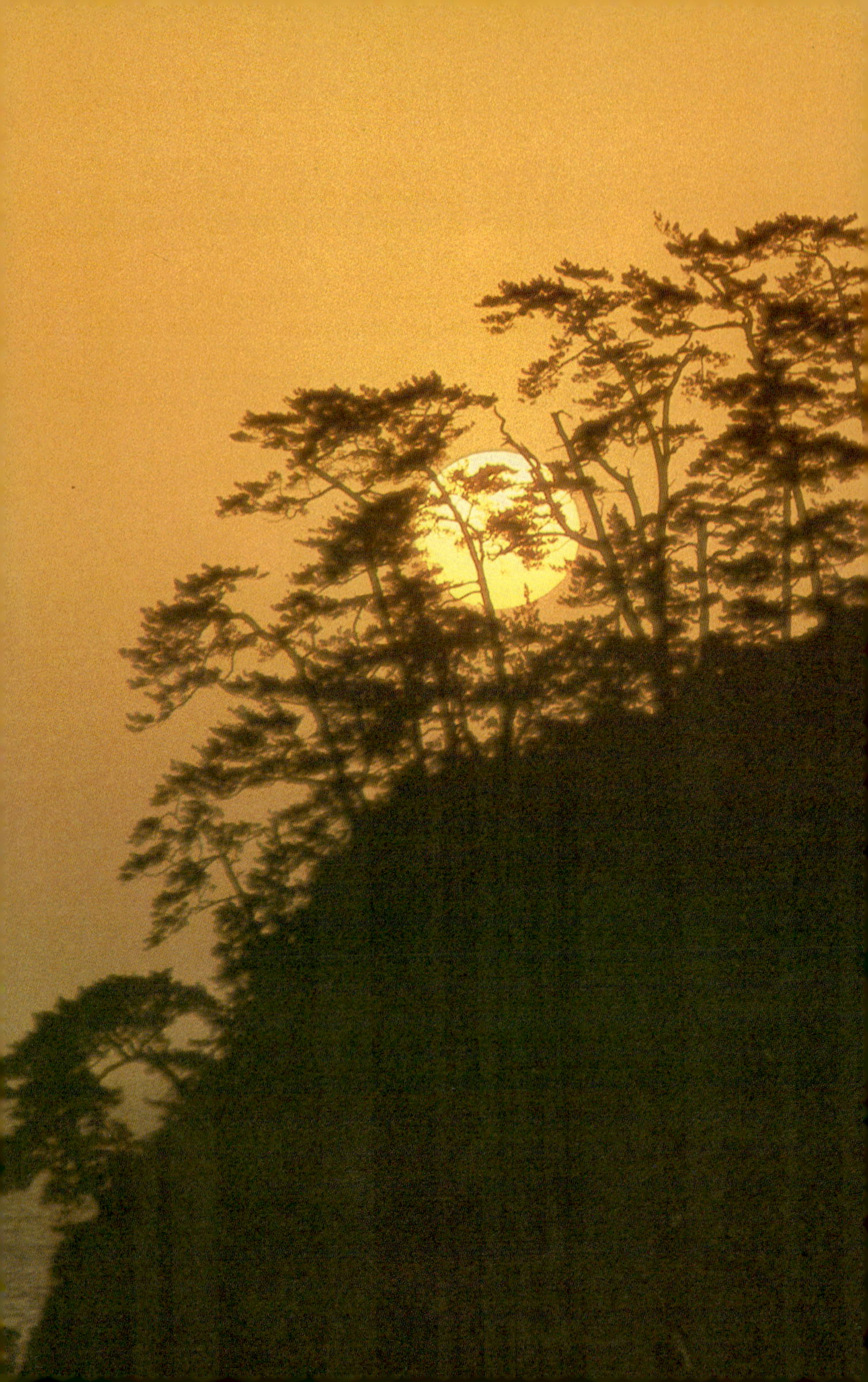

remote and underdeveloped hamlets and villages in Kyushu (Itsuki for example, famous throughout Japan for its haunting lullaby, first sung by the daughters of penniless village families who were sent while still children as nursemaids to the neighbouring towns).

Kumamoto City is dominated by the largest castle in Kyushu, the last castle in Japan to withstand a medieval-style siege. This occurred during the Satsuma Rebellion of 1877, when a garrison of 4,000 men held out for more than a month and a half against the much larger rebel army of Saigo Takamori (see Kagoshima, below). Their success is a testatment to the strength of Japanese military architecture, a strength visible in the massive stone walls that remain. The donjon, rebuilt in 1960 of ferroconcrete, houses a display of items connected with the siege.

A delicacy of Kumamoto is raw horsemeat, called *ba-zashi* or, more euphemistically, *sakura* (cherry). This is available in many of the city's restaurants but should be sampled only in those that specialize in it.

Mount Aso (5,223 feet or 1,592 metres) lies some 25 miles (40 km) west of Kumamoto City and is the centre of the national park that bears its name. Its chief peaks have been thrust up in the middle of the largest crater on earth (once the active mouth of a single massive volcano). The walls of this crater, spectacularly discernable from the peaks it encircles, form an oval 50 miles (80 km) in circumference. The crater is large enough to contain three complete townships, including several hot spring resorts, chief among which is Aso Onsen, though the higher spas, especially Yunotani, tend to be more picturesque.

The national park extends northward to include Mount Kuju (5,863 feet or 1,787 metres) and the high plateaus that surround it, too high to irrigate for rice cultivation, but which provide pasture for cattle or have been planted with tangerines.

Kagoshima and Sakurajima

Though Kagoshima Prefecture has the lowest per capita income in all Japan, the city of Kagoshima is among the most relaxing and eye-pleasing cities in the country. It is situated on Kagoshima Bay opposite the magnificent hulk of Mount Sakurajima, an active volcano 3,668 feet (1,118 metres) high, which completely dominates both city and bay. The mountain was an island until 1914 when, in a tremendous eruption, it spewed out enough lava to form a bridge between itself and the mainland.

Kagoshima city has wide, palm-planted boulevards and has attracted or encouraged very traditional industries: silk, pottery, and the production of *shochu*, a liquor made from either rice or potato which, south of Kumamoto, is a more common tipple than sake.

The Satsuma Peninsula on which Kagoshima stands is famous for two types of pottery: a colourfully painted variety called simply Satsuma, and a coarser, black-glazed variety called Black Satsuma. One of the best kilns on the peninsula is at Naeshirogawa, west of Kagoshima, where the potters (who are not nearly so visited by tourists as those of, say, Koishiwara in Fukuoka prefecture) are sometimes willing to demonstrate techniques.

Historically, Kagoshima is of considerable interest. It was here that the first Christian missionary, St Francis Xavier, landed in 1549, and it is a measure of the independence of the Satsuma clan that the lord of the province gave Xavier permission to preach without consulting either court or shogun. The independent spirit of Satsuma has become legendary, thanks largely to the exploits of Kagoshima's most famous native son, the charismatic Saigo Takamori (1827-1877). Saigo, one of the leading figures in the imperial restoration of 1868, later rose in rebellion against the new government and eventually committed suicide after being wounded on Shiroyama Hill in Kagoshima City (now a shrine to his memory). Despite his rebellion, Saigo is widely regarded as the last of the true samurai, embodying the qualities of modesty, loyalty, steadfastness and valour that were essential parts of the old warrior code.

Miyazaki and Mount Kirishima

Miyazaki City, in southwestern Kyushu, is the administrative capital of Miyazaki Prefecture and a good base for exploring both the subtropical coastline of this part of the island (particularly south of the city) and the hot springs, peaks and lakes of Mount Kirishima (5,577 feet or 1,700 metres), the central attraction of the Kirishima-Yaku National Park.

The area around Miyazaki is of particular interest to archaeologists since some of the earliest artifacts in Japanese history have been found here. These include the nearly 400 mounds at Saitobaru to the north and the various clay figures on exhibition in the museum of the Miyazaki Shrine. A less specialized attraction of the city is its air, reputedly the cleanest of any city in Japan — though this is tempered by Miyazaki's reputation for recording also the heaviest rainfall.

The coast between Aoshima, a small island joined to the mainland by a bridge, and Cape Toi is particularly pleasing and, unlike much of the Japanese coastline, affords good swimming.

The Kirishima-Yaku National Park, like that of Aso, is mainly famous for its hot springs centred on a still partly active volcano. If the park lacks the spectacular features of Aso's huge crater or Sakurajima seen from across Kagoshima Bay, it compensates with its wealth and variety of plants and trees, making a visit in autumn especially worthwhile. Kirishima Spa, just across the boundary with Kagoshima Prefecture, is a collection of more than a dozen hot springs situated at high altitude in pleasant hiking country.

Mt Aso (5, 257 ft), Kyoshi

Beppu

Beppu is an absolute mecca for hot spring enthusiasts. It is the single most famous spa in Japan and, as a result, is also the most commercially developed. Few visitors to Kyushu would think of missing it, and the vast number of hotels, ryokans and bath houses in the city could almost cater to the entire island's tourist population.

There are eight separate spas known collectively as Beppu, and together they boast almost 4,000 different springs, geysers, fissures and other openings. Nine types of thermal water have been analysed, mostly containing iron carbonate, sulphur and salt, and ranging in temperature as they emerge from the ground between 100°F and 212°F (37°C and 100°C) (the temperatures are of course adjusted for bathing).

Among Beppu's unique attractions are its mud and sand baths (the sand bath consists in being buried up to the neck on a hot beach) and its 'hells', which are the points where the thermal water issues most spectacularly from the ground, sometimes milky white or simply the colour of bubbling brown mud.

Connoisseurs spend days at a time strolling in the light cotton kimonos lent them by their ryokans from bath house to bar to hell to bath house and back to hell again. It is a no doubt healthy, though somewhat enervating, exercise.

Bathing in spas, Beppu

North of Beppu, in the town of Usa, stands the Usa Shrine, the most sacred in Kyushu. With its red lacquered buildings in their thickly wooded setting, it is known for its elegance rather than its awesomeness.

Okinawa

Some 60 islands form the Okinawa chain lying between the southern tip of Kyushu and the north of Taiwan. It is the only part of Japan that has anything close to a tropical climate, and still shows traces of its past independence.

Still known alternatively by its old name, Ryukyu, the island grouping was an active trading state in the middle ages, ruled by a dynasty of Confucian monarchs. Under the loose protection of China, to which it paid tribute, the Ryukyu kingdom followed a policy of unarmed neutrality, and its sailors and traders roved the seas of Asia.

This independence, or Chinese orientation, virtually ended in 1609 when a Japanese army from the Satsuma fiefdom in Kagoshima invaded and annexed the Ryukyu Islands. In 1879 the Meiji government formally incorporated the islands into Japanese territory.

The subsequent years saw much tragedy. The overcrowded, comparatively poor islands became important bases for Japan's expansion in Asia. When the tide turned, the main island, which is also called Okinawa, was devastated by a fierce three-month battle between United States forces and Japanese troops who mounted a suicidal defence. Military and civilian casualties are estimated at over 150,000 killed, mostly local people. The island remained under United States jurisdiction long after the Allied occupation of Japan ended and were returned to Japan only in 1972 to become the 47th prefecture. A United States marine division, an airforce base, and navy docks remain.

Naha, the capital of Okinawa prefecture, is a small city at the southern end of the main island, linked by air and sea with Japanese cities and several foreign points. It is also the hub of a network of ferries and feeder air routes to the smaller islands. While the war damage left little of its ancient architecture, an impressive Chinese-style gate remains and the city is the home of many experts in traditional Okinawan textile and ceramic making.

Ishigaki is one of the southernmost cluster of the Okinawan islands, at the same latitude as northern Taiwan. A sizable island covered with sugar cane, rain forest, pine groves and she-oaks, Ishigaki has many villages of the traditional type. Houses are strongly built of a local wood, with roof tiles cemented down in a strikingly attractive way, and surrounded by coral walls — all to withstand the typhoons which frequently hit Okinawa in late summer. Ishigaki and many other Okinawan islands are surrounded by coral reefs to rival the Great Barrier Reef of Australia.

Iriomote, a short ferry ride from Ishigaki, is virtually deserted, but contains much in its tropical jungles and rivers to interest the physically active explorer, including a unique species of wild cat.

The Island of Hokkaido

Many Japanese people regard a trip to Hokkaido as the next best thing to going abroad. The island, formerly called Ezo, was not universally recognized as a part of Japan until the 1860s. Before that, most of it belonged to the Ainu, the earliest inhabitants of Japan who had been driven there by the close of the 9th century. It is too far north for rice to play a predominant part in its economy, it has comparatively few cherry trees (a national symbol) and no distinct rainy season. The Russian island of Sakhalin is visible from its northernmost cape and very un-Japanese icefloes graze stretches of its coast in winter.

Hokkaido is not really a destination for the traveller with limited time whose chief interests are old Japanese temples or typical Japanese communities. Its main attractions are natural, not human. Much of the island is untouched by industry and the population density is far less than in

THE ISLAND OF HOKKAIDO

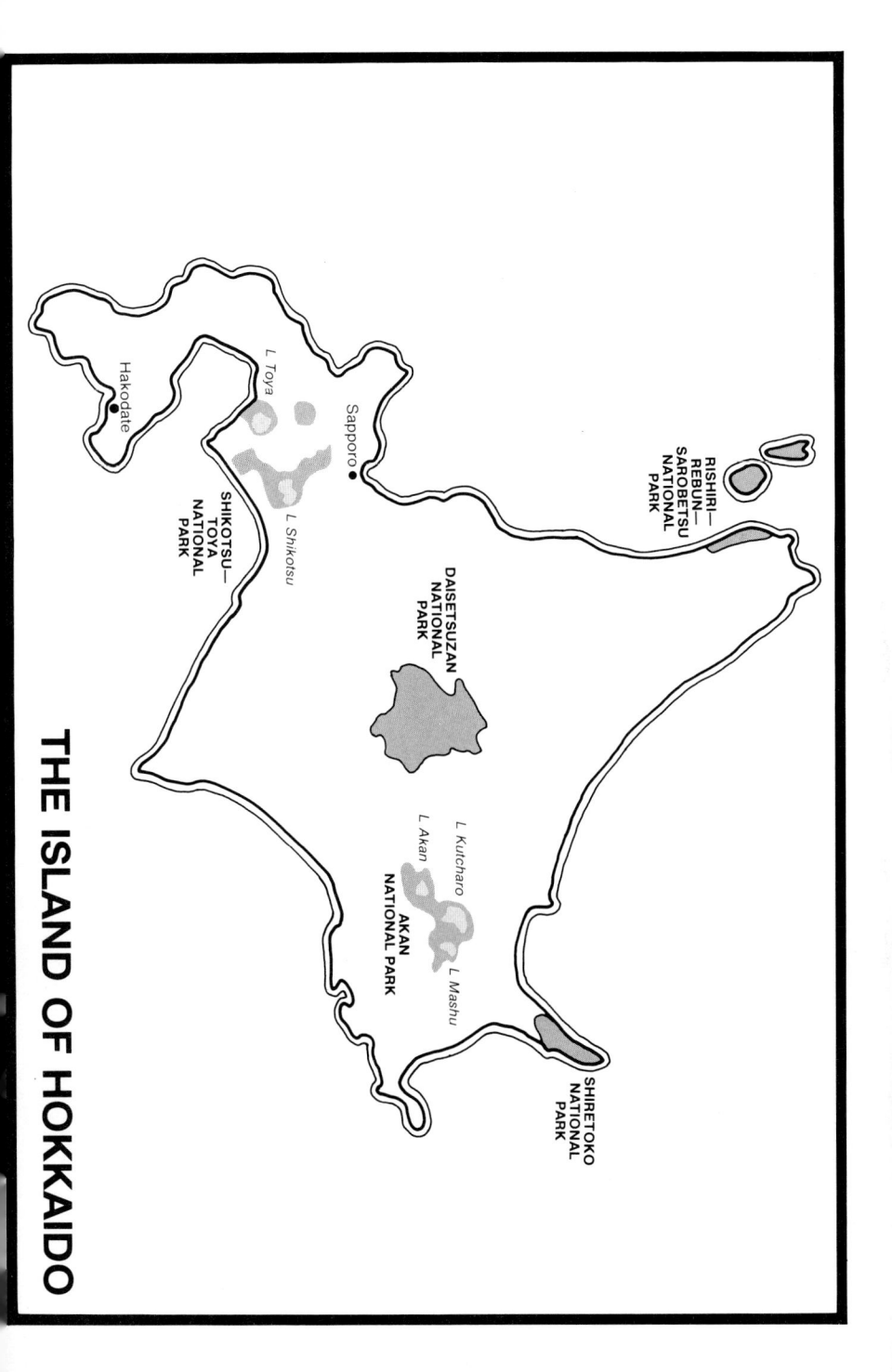

the rest of Japan (5 percent of the total population spread over about one-fifth of the total land area).

Sapporo

Sapporo is the administrative capital of Hokkaido and was the site of the 1972 Winter Olympics. The city was planned and built virtually from scratch in the 1870s, when it was decided to 'colonize' Hokkaido in earnest. Its streets and blocks were laid out on a rectangular pattern that was thought to be progressive and 'American'. Sapporo thus lacks the haphazard quality of many Japanese cities and, as a result, some would say, lacks also their charm.

A good way to orient oneself is from the observation platform of Sapporo Tower, 230 feet (70 metres) above street level. The regular design of the city is discernible at a glance. One might then stroll along Sapporo's most famous shopping street, Tanuki-koji (Racoon Dog Alley). This was once the centre of the city's nightlife and earned its name from the women who worked there and who proved able to spirit away their clients' cash quite as magically as any racoon dog (an animal renowned in Japanese folklore for its trickery). Today the alley is a far more innocent place and those in search of nocturnal adventures are better off in Susukino, a couple of blocks southeast.

The old Sapporo brewery is worth a visit, partly because the red-brick buildings, which date from 1876, are pleasant in themselves, but mainly because they have now been converted into Japan's largest beer hall. (Sapporo lies on the same degree of latitude as Milwaukee, the beer capital of the United States.) Here, at the Biiruen, Hokkaido's 'foreignness' is clearly in evidence. Beer is spelt *bier*, the main item of food on the menu is a mutton dish called 'Genghis Khan', and the lavatories are marked *Herren* and *Damen*.

Foreignness is conspicuous at the city's agricultural college too. It was founded in 1876 by an American, Dr William Smith Clark, whose bust is to be seen there, and whose parting words to his students, 'Boys be ambitious,' have become one of Japan's best-loved quotations.

Hakodate

Unlike Sapporo, a city from its earliest days, Hakodate began life as a fishing village and grew to fill out its natural boundaries. The city is, in fact, a small peninsula jutting out into the Tsugaru Strait and terminating in the bulk of Mount Hakodate, which helps form its impressive natural harbour. It was one of the earliest Japanese settlements on Hokkaido and one of the first ports to be opened to foreign commerce (in 1859).

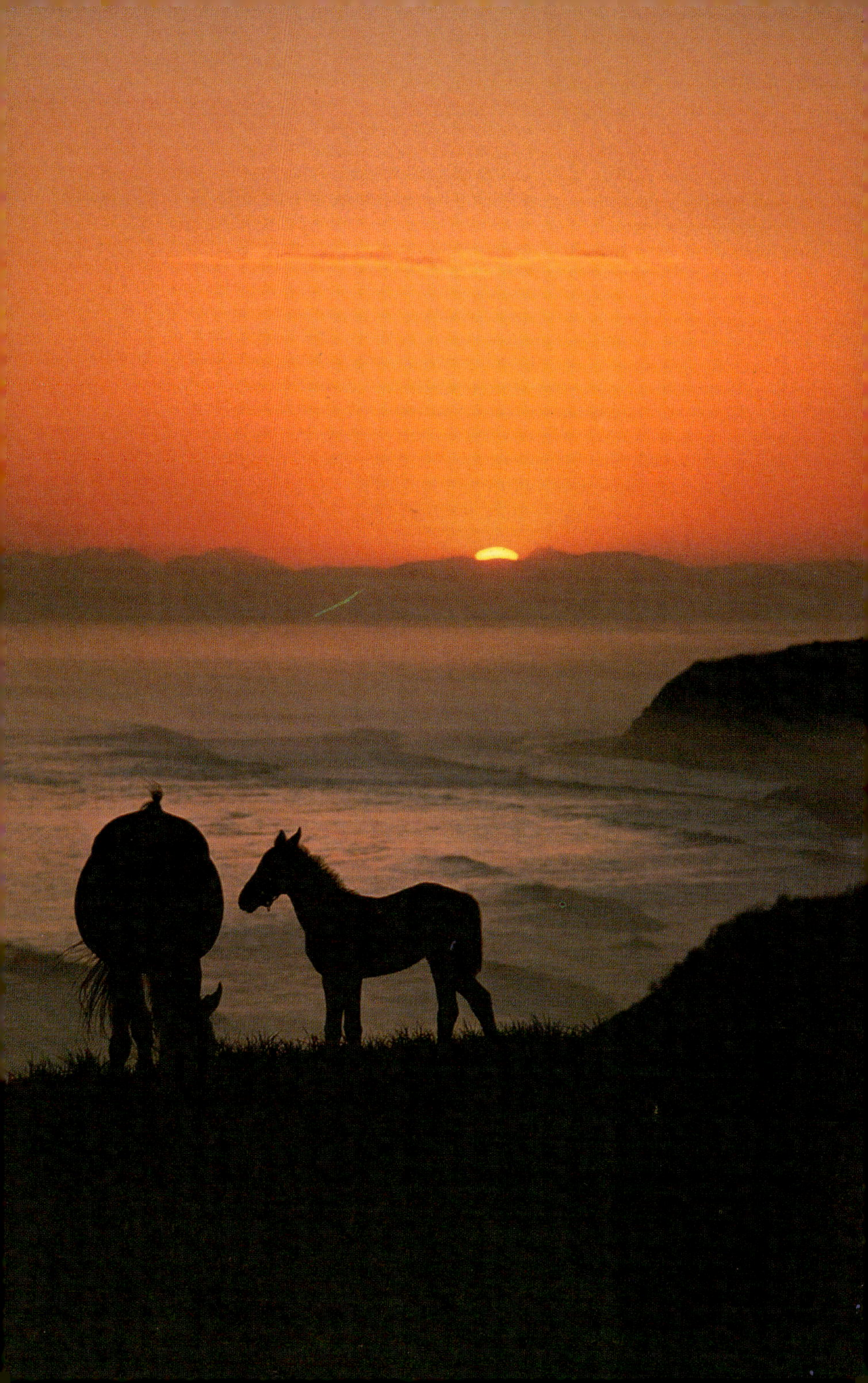

The view of the city from the top of Mount Hakodate (1,099 feet or 335 metres), which is accessible by bus or more interestingly by ropeway, is breathtaking, especially at night. It should perhaps be the visitor's first objective since, in daylight at least, it provides a perfect orientation.

Hakodate has a liveliness and a casual quality that Sapporo lacks. Its principal industry is fishing and there is often a good deal of bustling market activity going on in the streets just south of the station. It is also one of the last cities in Japan to retain as its main means of public transport a streetcar system, which, in the view of many, adds to its distinction.

Again, many Japanese visitors are struck by the 'foreign' atmosphere that pervades the city. One of the most intriguing landmarks visible from Mount Hakodate is a Byzantine-style Russian Orthodox church and there is a Trappist convent nearby (founded in 1898), whose secluded inmates manufacture one of Hakodate's most popular souvenirs, called Trappist cookies.

Visitors may prefer to stay at the nearby hot spring resort of Yunokawa, the terminus of one of the streetcar lines. Yunokawa is among the oldest and best-known spas in Hokkaido, but its easy access has led to overdevelopment and it is now a mass of western-style hotels.

Also worth a visit are the remains of the 'Star Fort,' the first western-style fortress in Japan and the scene of a month-long siege that took place during the collapse of the feudal government in 1868.

National Parks of Hokkaido

Whatever the attractions of Sapporo and Hakodate, the wise visitor to Hokkaido will spend less time in the cities than among the lakes and mountains of the island which comprise some of Japan's loveliest and least spoiled scenery. Five areas have been designated national parks and the advantages of visiting these are the restrictions on industrial encroachment which have kept them unspoiled, and the ready availability of accommodation, albeit often simple.

The most easily accessible of the parks from either Sapporo or Hakodate is Shikotsu-Toya, which includes two lakes, several active volcanoes (one of which, Mount Usu, erupted spectacularly in 1977, and another of which, Showa Shinzan, was formed as recently as 1945) and a number of hot spring resorts. Of these, the best known is Toyako Onsen on the western shore of Lake Toya, but it is also the most commercialized. Visitors in search of a quieter, more authentic spa might find Marukoma Onsen on the northern shore of Lake Shikotsu more to their taste (there is only one large Japanese-style inn there). The stretch of seacoast south of Lake Shikotsu is also interesting since Noboribetsu (another major hot spring resort) is situated there, and at Shiraoi there is an Ainu village of recent origin which offers visitors a somewhat contrived glimpse of the lifestyle of this aboriginal race, a different race altogether from the Japanese and one that has become almost extinct through intermarriage.

Further northeast, in the middle of the island, lies the largest of the parks, Daisetsuzan (literally Great Snowy Mountains). Here the landscape is at its finest and the mountains (several over 6,500 feet or 2,000 metres) are the tallest in Hokkaido. They are also among the haunts of the Hokkaido brown bear, Japan's largest wild animal. Probably the best base from which to explore Daisetsuzan is Sounkyo Onsen, a hot spring resort beautifully situated in the Sounkyo Gorge and now easily reached from the city of Asahikawa by means of the Daisetsu highway. There are other good hot springs in the park too(many of them less commercially developed) and Daisetsuzan is ideally suited for hikers and other outdoor enthusiasts.

Further east lies the Akan National Park, the main features of which are its three lakes — Kutcharo, the largest, Mashu and Lake Akan itself. All three are surrounded by forested hills and all have hot spring resorts on their shores which, again, provide the most convenient accommodation. Lake Akan is particularly interesting for two reasons. It is the home of a curious spherical water weed called *marimo* to which, for reasons that can only be guessed at, the Japanese have developed a sentimental attachment. (It is the lakeside resort's chief souvenir and the government has declared it a 'Special Natural Monument'.) The weed also features prominently in the October Marimo Festival mounted by the small Ainu community who live in the resort (Akankohan), and are the other focus of interest. Their 'village' is a collection of carefully rustic souvenir shops and a house-like theatre where, for a fee, the visitor can watch a group of them pretending to be at home. Hokkaido's remaining two national parks are both situated on the coast and thus offer a completely different environment, though one just as wild and often as interesting. Neither is as developed as the inland parks and they are both more difficult to get to and provide less in the way of accommodation and tourist facilities. Trips to them should really only be considered if the visitor likes rough country and has plenty of time to spare.

Shiretoko National Park comprises virtually the whole of the mountainous Shiretoko Peninsula, which juts out like a pointing finger into the Sea of Okhotsk opposite the Soviet-occupied island of Kunashiri, one of four such islands whose return the Japanese government is demanding. Its unspoiled vegetation and the seabirds that nest on its steep cliffs are magnets for naturalists. Of all the regions comprising the Hokkaido parks, Shiretoko is the least developed.

The other coastal park (Rishiri-Rebun-Sarobetsu) comprises the flat plain south of the city of Wakkanai, near the northernmost cape of Hokkaido, and the two offshore islands of Rebun and Rishiri. The Sarobetsu plain is

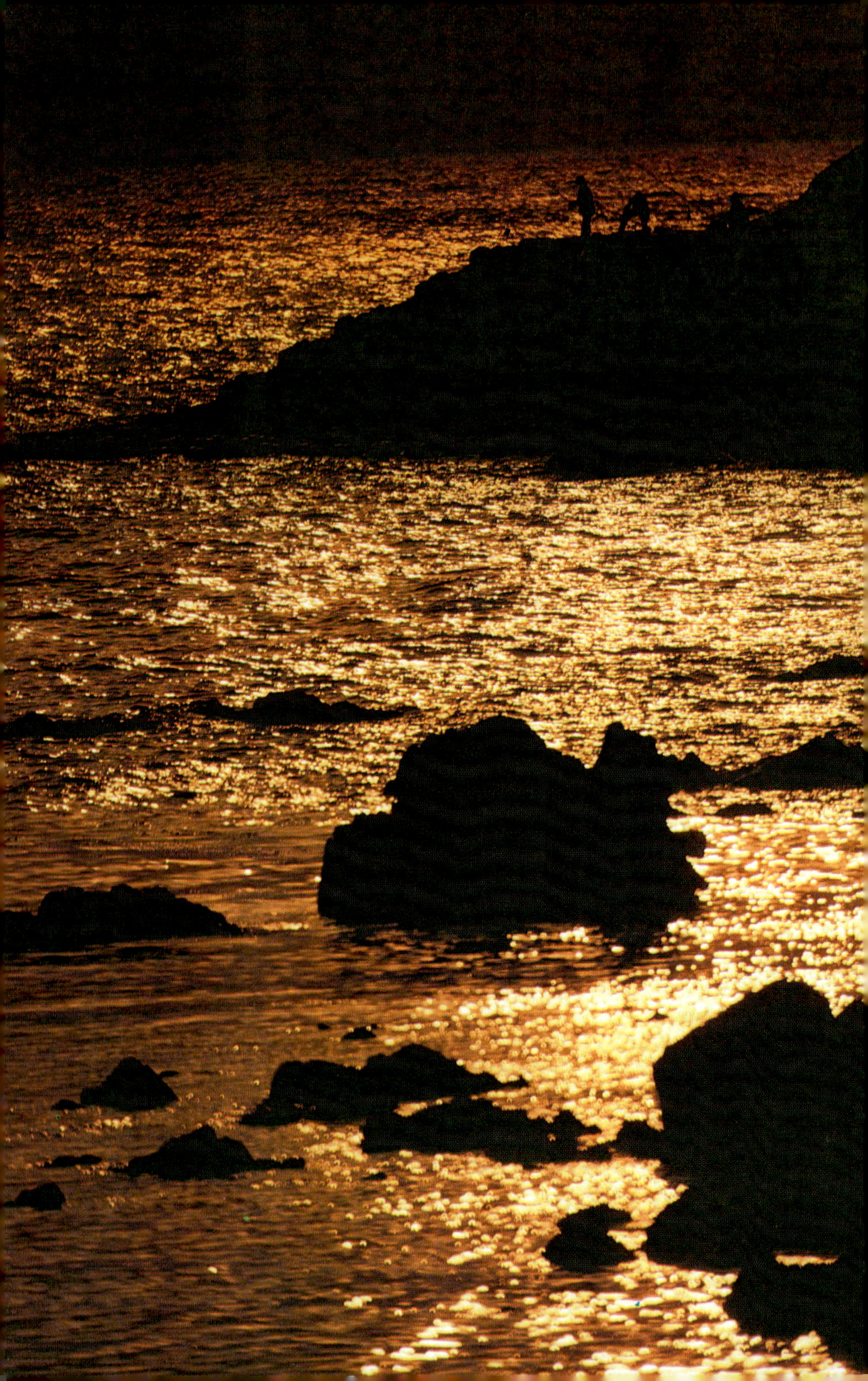

famous for its flowers, while the landscape of the two islands, though attractive, is rather desolate. Rishiri is volcanic. Rebun is a bleak, though friendly place where walking, camping and fishing are the attractions. There is an eight-hour hiking course along the west coast of Rebun (not served by a road) which only the hardy should attempt.

Recommended Reading

This volume is intended as an introduction to travel in Japan. The most informative book available is Ian McQueen's *Japan, A Travel Survival Kit* (Lonely Planet Publications, South Yarra, Australia 1981). Written for the independent traveller with a tight budget but unlimited time, the 'kit' has a great deal of practical information. The most accomplished guide to Japan for the discerning traveller is Peter Popham's "Insiders Guide to Japan" (CFW Publications Ltd. Hong Kong). Both authors do assume that their readers are interested in Japan as a whole, rather than just tourist attractions. By way of contrast *Japan 1983* by Robert C Fisher (Fisher Travel Guides Incorporated, New York 1982) is for more conventional vistors who have some money, but not a great deal of time. The books lists major hotels and restaurants.

Nagel's Encyclopedia-Guide Japan (Nagel Publishers, Geneva, Paris and Munich 1979) is now so out-of-date (despite its putative publication date) that it has become something of a classic. It is beautifully written. *The New Official Guidebook Japan* (Japan National Tourist Organization, Tokyo 1975) is more a reference work than a guide in its own right, though it can be used to advantage with one of the other books listed above. Japan Air Lines have published *Japan Unescorted: A Practical Guide to Discovering Japan On Your Own* by James K Weatherly (1982) which has useful information on ten different cities.

The specialized travel literature is of a higher standard than the general books, but there is still no comprehensive guide to Tokyo. Don Briggs has written *Tokyo, A Confidential Guide to the Greatest* (Don Briggs Productions, Tokyo 1978), an entertaining collection of amazing facts about the capital, linked together with atrocious puns. *Foot-loose in Tokyo* by Jean Pearce (Weatherhill, New York and Tokyo 1976) is a very good rambler's guide to the environs of the 29 overground railway stations of the Yamanote Line. *Around Tokyo: A Day-Tripper's Guide* by John Turrent and Jonathan Lloyd-Owen (The Japan Times Limited, Tokyo 1982) has selective coverage of the capital and the Kanto region. The city of Yokohama has published an excellent large-format volume entitled *Yokohama, Portrait of a City from its Port Opening to the 21st Century* (Yokohama, 1982). Michael Cooper has written an excellent guide entitled *Exploring Kamakura* (Weatherhill, New York and Tokyo 1979) which is essential reading for visitors to that city.

The standard work on the northeast of Honshu is *Exploring Tohoku* by Jan Brown (Weatherhill, New York and Tokyo 1982) though the text is heavily weighted towards the northern part of this region. *In and Around Sendai* by James Vardaman, Margaret Garner and Ruth Vergin (Keyaki No Machi Company Limited, Sendai 1981) has useful information about Miyagi and Iwate prefectures *Kanazawa* by Ruth Stevens is appropriately published by the Society to Introduce Kanazawa to the World (Kanazawa 1979).

Kyoto is served by two excellent books, which are well worth acquiring before a visit to the old capital. *Kyoto, A Contemplative Guide* by Gouverneur Mosher (Tuttle, Rutland, Vermont and Tokyo 1964) is a selective, in-depth introduction to the history and culture of the city. *A Guide to the Gardens of Kyoto* by Marc Treib and Ron Herman (Shufunotomo, Tokyo 1980) covers many historic buildings as well as the gardens. While explaining the aesthetic principles of Japanese garden design, it also has much practical information.

The adventurous traveller will require a compass and a good set of maps. The latter are not easy to come by. The Japanese are erratic, often indifferent cartographers. Many of the free maps given to tourists are well nigh useless. *Teikoku's Complete Atlas of Japan* (Teikoku-Shoin Company Limited, Tokyo 1982) is a slim book useful for working out itineraries. The best map of the capital is published by the same company: *Tokyo: Red Series 1 (Falk Plan)*. The best map of *Kyoto*, drawn to a scale of 1:25,000, is published by the Geographical Survey Institute (Japan 1981) and includes a floral calendar and a list of annual events.

Takashi Ishihara has drawn a series of beautiful 'bird's eye view' maps of *Kamakura, Nara, Kobe, Tenri,* and *Kyoto* (which is in two parts). These are also published by the Geographical Survey Institute (Japan 1981).

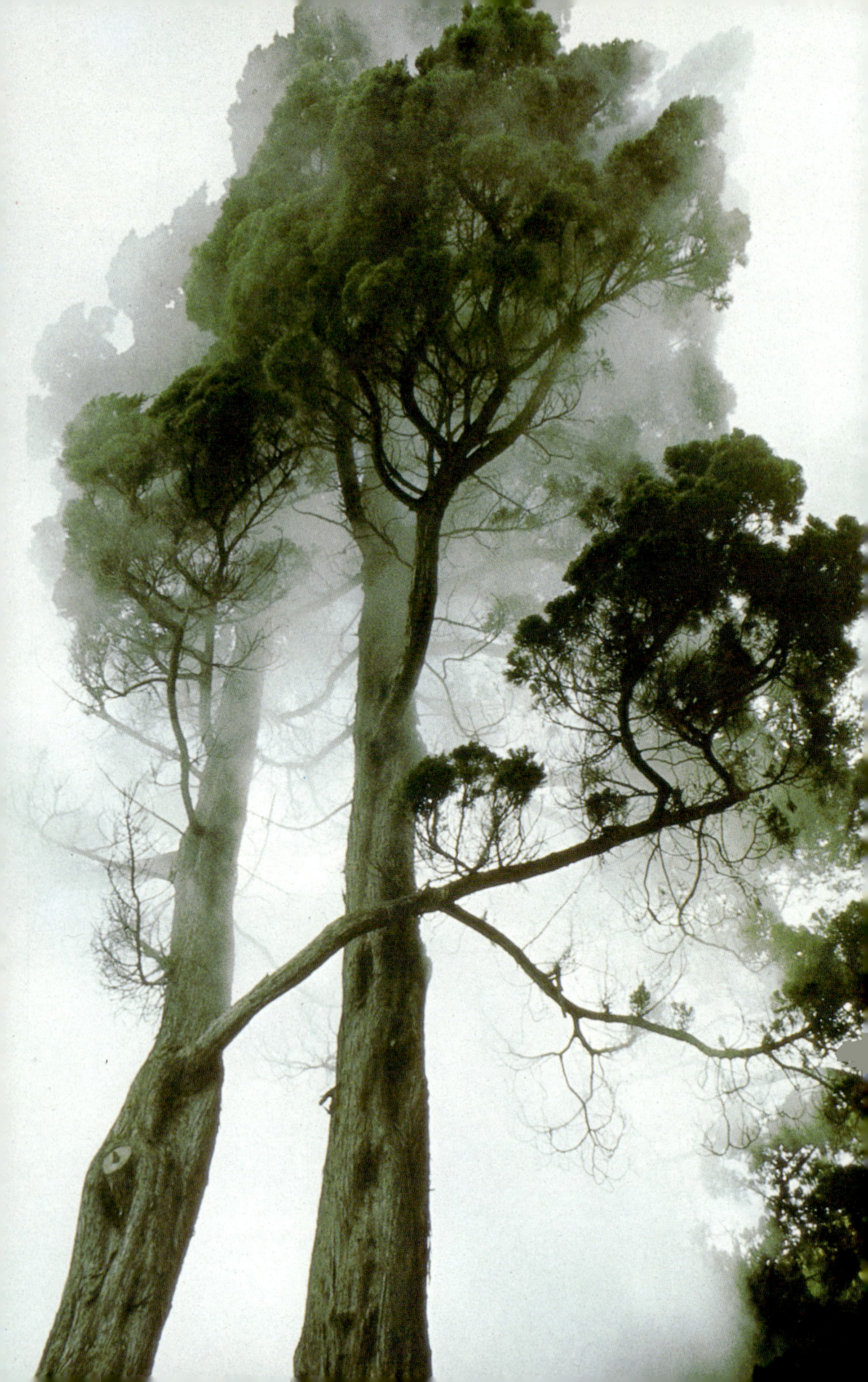

Appendix
Inns, Hotels and Other Accommodation

Staying at a Japanese inn or hotel is an essential part of the Japan experience — or it should be. Foreign visitors are the guests of the Japanese people at all times, but especially in the place where they are staying.

The inns and hotels offer fine service at such a wide range of prices and in such a variety of forms as to suit almost any pocket or life-style. Businessmen may prefer to stay at large international hotels with telex machines and all-night coffee shops. In Tokyo the big hotels are generally the best located and most convenient places to stay. Outside the capital foreign travellers will be drawn to the *ryokan*, the Japanese inns, some luxurious, some frugal, that offer a real involvement in Japanese life. They are among the world's most delightful hostelries.

Foreign tourists should book ahead if possible, through a travel agent or Japanese-speaking friend, or at least make a telephone call before arriving. (The tourist information centres do not officially make reservations, but will be able to give assistance, see page 20). Reservations should be confirmed if there is any chance of arriving late. Normally the price will be *per person*, not per room and the manager will need to know how many people there are and how many rooms are required. The price will include one or probably two meals, and sometimes travellers may be refused accommodation if they ask only for lodging.

The Japan National Tourist Organization now has a splendid free booklet entitled *The Tourist's Handbook: Practical Ways To Relieve Your Language Problems*, a large section of which is devoted to accommodation. It contains a list in both English and Japanese of all the basic questions a guest needs to ask, together with a choice of suitable answers. It can be used as a last resort when other forms of communication fail. (It should also be invaluable in making friends.)

One further thing should be noted. The Japanese lavatory is not at all like the western lavatory. There is no seat. There is NO seat. You squat. Anyone who can't, perhaps because of a stiff leg or a bad back, should check before booking whether the place selected has a western facility. The higher the price the more likely it is to have a western lavatory.

Japanese Inns (Ryokan) There are 90,000-odd ryokan in Japan, most of them run as small family businesses. Only the exceptional ryokan is as large as a western-style hotel. They are similar in style to traditional Japanese houses. The rooms are furnished with *tatami* mats, sliding doors called *fusuma* (plain) and *shoji* (with paper windows). Everybody sits on the floor. Cushions called *zabuton* are used instead of chairs.

Arriving at the ryokan guests are taken to their room by a specially appointed maid and served green tea. This invariably middle-aged lady will later serve meals in the same room and in the evening come to spread out cotton quilts, called *futon*, on the floor. This is the Japanese bed. In the morning she will put away the quilts in a cupboard.

The maid also tells her guests when they may take a bath. Some inns will provide private bathrooms. These normally have small, upright tubs of the kind used in Japanese houses. You sit, instead of lying, with your chin on your knees.

The Way of the Japanese Inn: Rules of the House

One   You remove your shoes when entering the inn, and wear the slippers provided.
Two   You take off the slippers before treading on any of the mats.
Three *In the lavatory* you use the special slippers provided there, but never (horror of horrors) walk outside in them.
Four   You don't use any soap in the bath. You wash at a basin or have a shower first, and then soak in the bath afterwards.

Most ryokan however do not have private bathrooms. Japanese guests prefer to relax in large communal baths, if these are available, where they can stretch out and perhaps even enjoy a view of the garden. These baths are almost always segregated by sex (for those that are not see the following section about *onsen ryokan*). Equipped only with a small, but decorously (i.e. modestly) handled, porous towel called a *tenugui*, the guest enters the bathroom. He or she then washes at a basin or showers BEFORE entering the bath. Many people also wash after the bath.

Japanese tend to bathe at a higher temperature than most foreigners can stand. It is nevertheless bad manners to fill the bath with cold water when other guests are waiting their turn to soak. Foreign visitors should always try to bathe as late in the evening as possible, when the temperature should be lower anyway.

Ryokan vary enormously in price. The cheapest may only cost ¥5,500 per person per night without meals. The finest may charge up to ¥60,000 per person for the privilege of staying in the best rooms and eating the best Japanese food. Most of these ryokan have beautiful gardens; certain rooms will have their own private gardens attached. Generally speaking any ryokan charging more than ¥8,000 should be *very* pleasant to stay in.

The Japan National Tourist Organization provides information about two particular groups of Japanese inns. Their own *Japan Ryokan Guide* brochure has full details of about 300 members of the Japan Ryokan Association (JRA). The association consists of 2,373 of the finest ryokan in the country. Rates range from ¥8,000 per person to ¥60,000. Some of them have western-style rooms available.

On the other hand there is a new and growing organization of moderately priced ryokan called the Japanese Inn Group. Their leaflet, entitled *Hospitable and Economical* contains a booking form and is available from JNTO and their head office c/o Hiraiwa Ryokan, 314 Hayao-cho, Kaminoguchi-agaru, Ninomiyacho-dori, Kyoto 600, telephone (03) 822 2251. Sixty-six ryokan are listed, charging approximately ¥3,500 to ¥5,000 per person.

For budget travellers the TICs have lists of even cheaper inns and private houses offering accommodation to foreigners.

It should also be noted that it is quite permissable to ask for a discount in off-season. This is best done by simply and politely saying that your budget extends to a certain figure and no further. Inns are more likely to accept your offer if you agree to check out as early as possible on the morning of departure.

Hot Spring Inns (Onsen Ryokan) The inns with the most character are located at hot springs, sometimes in a large resort, sometimes isolated deep in the mountains. They are popular with Japanese guests who go there to rest and forget their worries. No one has anything much to do, and the inns have an exceptionally friendly atmosphere. They run the gamut from rustic simplicity and slight sleaziness to pure elegance.

The most interesting are invariably the most remote. In parts of northeast and central Honshu it is still possible to find *tojiba*, 'water healing places', consisting of old thatched-roofed dormitories built around a complex of baths, where it is possible to stay for as little as ¥400 a night. Rather like camping, guests cook for themselves, sometimes even gathering the food for themselves from the fields and streams. Mixed bathing is the rule rather than the exception — often in the open air — considered completely natural by the old farmers who are the main guests.

At the other end of the social spectrum there are exclusive ryokan in fashionable spas with every Japanese-style luxury and comfort, including the attentions of Japan's traditional lady entertainers, the *geisha*. The cost may well be a hundred times that of the simple tojiba.

More moderate in price are the large, almost mass-market onsen ryokan (sometimes called hotels) that are often advertized on television. These have opulent baths, floor shows, sometimes safari parks and a host of other unimaginable attractions.

Hotels No special introduction is necessary here to the hotels of Japan. They meet international standards in every conceivable way — except sometimes in the length of the baths, which tend to be on the short size. Service is excellent, both western and Japanese food is usually available. Western breakfast buffets are common.

There are hotels in cities, towns and resorts throughout Japan: their clientele is overwhelmingly Japanese. Hotel employees generally speak a little more English, however, than those at ryokan. The best hotels, some 339 of them, are members of the Japan Hotel Association. They include

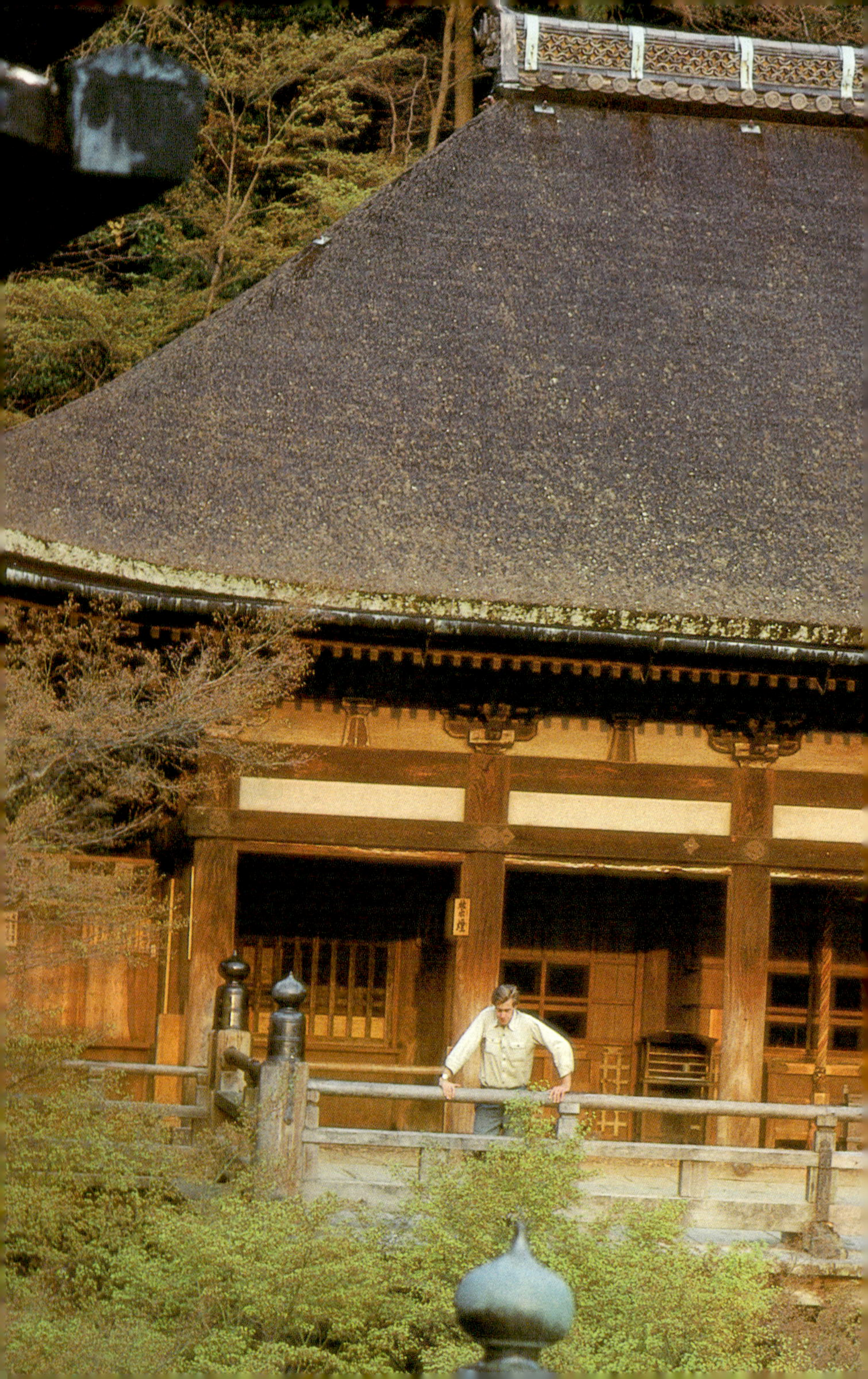

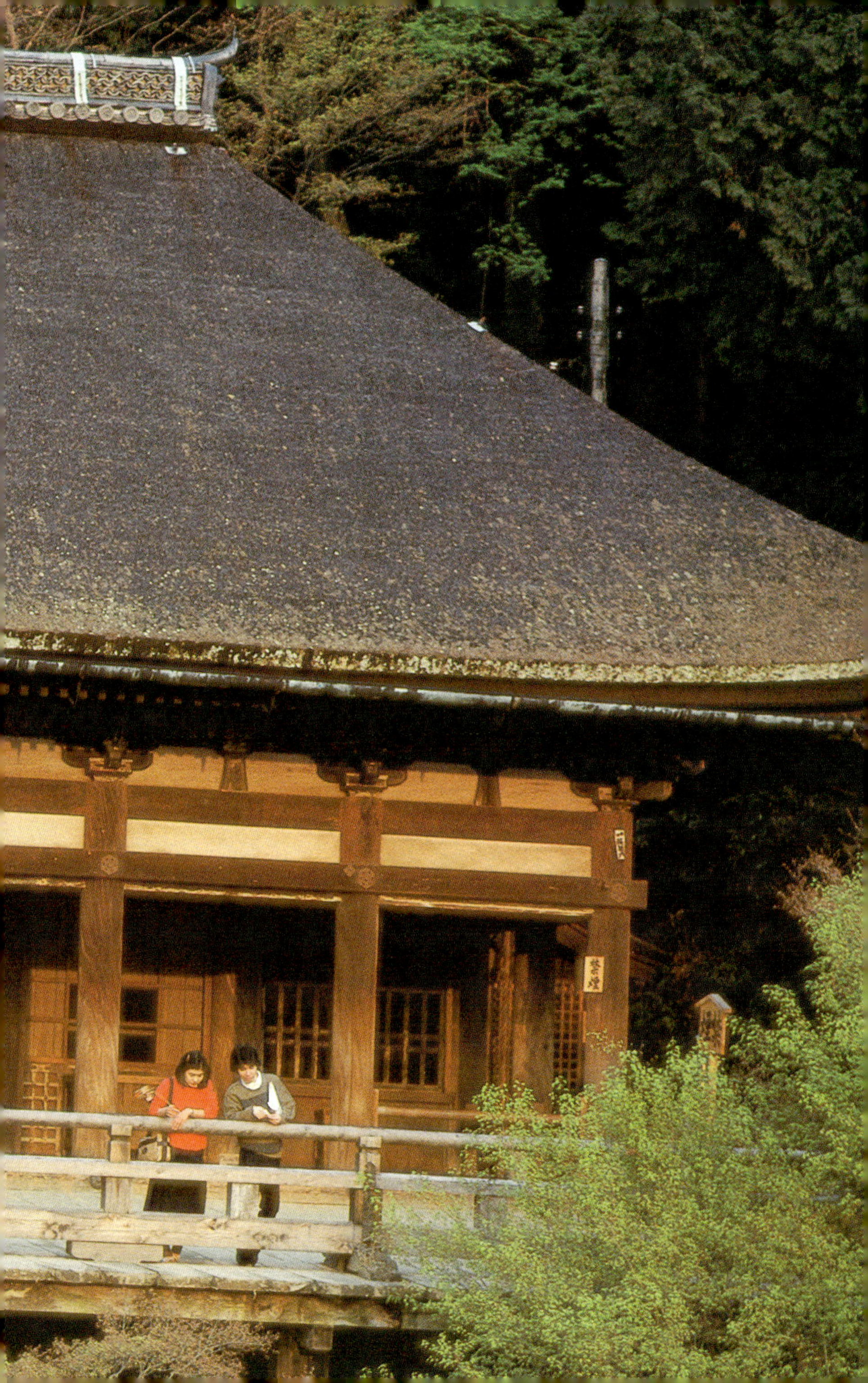

the large international hotels of the main cities, some of which are represented abroad. Travel agents should have details.

The price range for hotels is considerably narrower than that for Japanese inns: approximately ¥7,000 to ¥30,000 for a single room. Double rooms are a little more economical, on a per person basis. Meals are not included.

The Japan Travel Bureau (JTB) sells sets of hotel coupons. The scheme is called the 'Sunrise Super Saver' (SSS). The coupons, which can be used in 42 different cities in Japan, cost ¥45,500 for seven nights in single rooms or ¥77,000 for two people sharing a double room (prices to be held till the end of 1983).

Business Hotels As the name may possibly imply, these hotels have moderately priced rooms for travellers who merely want to stay the night. The rooms are small, check-out time is early and the hotel restaurant may just be a coffee shop. Prices range from around ¥4,000 per person to ¥7,000.

Love Hotels This uniquely Japanese form of accommodation offers fantasy and discretion. Much of the fantasy is on the outside. Some love hotels are shaped like ocean liners, some like gothic or baroque castles, French chateaux, Egyptian pyramids, the list is endless. One is surmounted by an enormous Statue of Liberty.

The discretion is found inside. Every effort is made to guarantee the anonymity of the couple staying there. A sum, from about ¥6,000 upwards, is passed through a curtained window to enable a couple to spend a night away from husbands, wives, or sometimes just to get away from the kids.

The best-known love hotel in Tokyo is the Hotel Meguro Emperor, 2-1-6 Shimo Meguro, Meguro-ku, telephone (03) 494 1211.

Minshuku Amateur inns, *minshuku* are found all over Japan, but especially in picturesque villages. They are similar in atmosphere to the British bed and breakfast establishments. Minshuku are in fact ordinary houses, licensed to let a certain number of rooms to travellers. Prices are determined by local associations and rigidly adhered to. There are no discounts.

Some are very friendly, though in others the mistress of the house may be more frightened of making a *faux pas* than even her foreign guests. Meals are eaten in the guest's room, never with the family. The price per person for one night, breakfast and dinner is around ¥5,000.

Information may be obtained from the TICs or from the Japan Minshuku Association, 2-10-8 Hyakunin-cho, Shinjuku-ku, Tokyo 161, telephone (03) 317 8120.

National Vacation Villages These are large hotel and recreational complexes run by the government. There are 32 of them, all in national parks. The accommodation is very reasonable in price, ranging from ¥2,500 to ¥5,000 per person with two meals. In Japanese these are referred to as *kokumin kyuka mura*.

People's Lodges Also primarily in national parks, these are smaller and more like ryokan or minshuku than the vacation villages. Some, but not all, are publicly owned. Generally very friendly places, they are in relatively inaccessible parts of the country. Prices tend to be a little higher than those at minshuku. JTB can book both the lodges and vacation villages. In Japanese, people's lodges are called *kokumin shukusha*.

Pensions Despite the name, pensions are generally small hotels for people taking part in outdoor sports. Many of them are ski lodges. Similar to the people's lodges, they are 50 percent more expensive, 50 percent more comfortable. There are several hundred of them, spread throughout the country. Information is available at the TICs.

Youth Hostels It is a fact that more foreigners use youth hostels than any other form of accommodation in Japan. There are good reasons for this. Youth hostels are very cheap, Japan has 550 of them, the best network outside Europe, and it is possible to meet other foreign travellers by staying in them. Although the accommodation is basically in same-sex dormitories, couples can usually get a room to themselves unless the hostel is full.

The disadvantages should also be noted. Woken up early in the morning, the hosteller has to be out between 10 am and 3 pm, then back in the hostel by 9 pm. Hostellers do their own washing-up after meals. In theory it is only possible to stay for three consecutive nights at any one hostel.

They vary enormously in terms of atmosphere and friendliness. The best ones, often purpose-built and managed by enthusiastic young people, are usually far off in the countryside, and difficult to find. The worst, mainly in the cities and towns, are down-at-heel ryokan that prefer hostellers to guests. Others may be in temples, shrines or private houses.

Basic accommodation charges vary but will be less than ¥2,500 a night. Breakfast costs around ¥500 and dinner about ¥1,000; the food is always Japanese.

Foreign hostellers need a membership card issued by an organization belonging to the International Youth Hostel Federation, or an international guest card from the Japan Youth Hostels. The address of the national organization is Hoken Kaikan, 1-2 Sadohara-cho, Ichigaya, Shinjuku-ku, Tokyo 162, telephone (03) 269 5831.

Camping The finest views are not to be had from the rooms of luxury hotels, nor is that the place to hear the amazing dawn chorus of birdsong in the Japanese mountains. However camping is restricted. In many areas it is only possible to pitch a tent at designated places for which a fee of ¥200 or more is payable. Camping is only practicable for visitors who have their own transport.

Eating and Drinking

Opinion is divided on the question of whether the Japanese have a major cuisine. It is increasingly popular in the States and Europe, and the mild, delicate flavours of Japanese food clearly appeal to northern palates. Those who enjoy the rich, mellow tastes of the Mediterranean or China, or indeed the spicy foods of southern countries will find the subtlety of Japanese cuisine rather elusive at first. Much of this subtlety — almost mystique — is in the presentation. The Japanese are probably the only people to have elevated the very *appearance* of their food into an art form.

In fact the traditional diet of the Japanese islands is a remarkably healthy one. Even today when the diet has been adulterated with milk and cheese, pizzas and hamburgers, fat consumption is still less than half that in western countries. (Lack of fat is also, of course, the reason why Japanese succumb to alcohol more easily than foreigners.)

There are two basic styles of Japanese cooking, that of Osaka and Kyoto (or Kansai) and that of the Tokyo area (or Kanto). Kansai food is more delicate and subtle in flavour (according to Osaka opinion), more insipid (according to Tokyo opinion) than Kanto food. The Kanto taste is undoubtedly stronger and more salty.

Foreigners are always surprised to find how many well-known Japanese dishes have been invented very recently or are of foreign origin. There is tremendous dynamism in the world of Japanese food, which is still in a phase of rapid development. Innovation alone makes the national cuisine one of the world's most interesting schools of cooking. (All this makes the Kansai-Kanto debate seem rather academic.)

Japanese eateries are the most specialized to be found anywhere. So much so that you decide what you are going to eat *before* you go to the restaurant. Most are very small, with limited menus that are in complete contrast to the extended lists of foods available in a typical large Chinese restaurant. There are in the region of 700,000 eating and drinking establishments in Japan, which is why this volume contains few specific recommendations. Instead of relentlessly tracking down particular restaurants, the independent traveller is better off learning to recognize the *kind* of eating or drinking house he is looking for.

The first thing to look for is the *noren*. This is a cotton curtain, which hangs in front of the door when the restaurant is open. When the place is closed it hangs *behind* the door. All but the cheapest Japanese eating and drinking places have them, also old-fashioned Japanese shops and some Chinese restaurants. Other foreign restaurants don't have them.

Most cheap to moderately expensive eating establishments display plastic (originally wax) models of their dishes in the window — a boon to bewildered foreigners. Ironically these were introduced in the last century to show off exotic and unfamiliar western foods to the Japanese. Restaurants without plastic models are invariably more expensive when it comes to the final bill. The dividing line is very roughly around ¥2,600 to ¥3,600 per person.

Visitors should be on the look-out for *table d'hôte* lunches, sometimes dinners, called *teishoku* (pronounced *tay-shock-u*). These save money and obviate ordering separate dishes. Sometimes there are more than one. Similar special offers of snacks (coffee and cake, coffee and sandwiches) are called *setto* from the English word *set*.

After the meal payment is normally made direct to the cashier and not at the table (no tipping!). At that time any visitor unsure of where he has been can always ask for *matchi*, a box of matches which invariably will have the address and telephone number of the establishment. Some restaurants have name cards.

Foreign restaurants are like Japanese girls with dyed-red hair, of more interest to the Japanese themselves than to visitors from abroad. However the Japanese treat French food with great respect and the taste is fairly authentic. There are many patisseries, often doubling as coffee shops. There are good restaurants, especially in the capital. Some are interesting places where the food is French, and excellent, but the setting is entirely Japanese in style. (These are difficult to find, but one that can be recommended is *Kusunoki-tei*, 28-32 Hongo 1-chome, Bunkyo-ku, Tokyo, telephone (03) 813 7218.)

Italian restaurants are ubiquitous and of low quality. Real Italian tomato taste is rare, the spaghetti is over-cooked and in places where pizza bread is not yet made, they offer 'pizza toast' instead.

Chinese food is a disaster. Those familiar with true Chinese cuisine will probably be unable to recognize the Japanese variety. Any visitor who remembers poor Chinese food in Brisbane, Bradford or the Badlands of South Dakota will be surprised to learn that the world's worst Chinese restaurant has been located in Yamagata Prefecture. Chinese restaurants tend to be very cheap, likewise Korean.

Really exotic food — Greek, Javanese, Czechoslovakian, Spanish, Indian, Mexican, Swedish, Thai, Bulgarian, Singaporean, Swiss, Persian and probably Hebridean — is cooked in restaurants in the fashionable sections of the capital.

Coffee shops, called *kissaten*, are the best places to nurse aching feet, write postcards or talk to new friends. A cup of the beverage in question (or alternatively black tea with milk and sugar) costs around ¥350 and entitles the customer to stay as long as he or she cares to. There is no hustling. The coffee is freshly-ground, freshly-made and usually quite strong. Weak coffee is called American. For a premium it is possible to select from a list of a dozen or so special coffees: Mocca, Brazilian, Blue Mountain (Jamaican), and Kilimanjaro (East African) are all popular and can be asked for in

English. Coffee in the best kissaten is charcoal roasted. Light meals are on the menu.

Japanese consider their coffee shops to be 'western' and accordingly feel comfortable with foreign customers. Some even give special discounts to foreigners who enhance the atmosphere of their establishments! For the most part they are peaceful, sober places where the customers are left in peace, their privacy respected.

Coffee shops have great charm, not merely convenience. Intriguing places, they represent, better than anything, the hybrid style of the new Japan. Eschewing the televisions that wreck the atmosphere in many restaurants, each kissaten is an experiment in interior design and music. Each one specializes in a particular kind of music: jazz, rock, techno-pop, *chanson*, and many others. There are ultra-serious classical music places where all the chairs face in the same direction and nobody talks. Others that publish a monthly programme of the records they intend to play. With an attention to detail clearly deriving from the traditional tea ceremony, many kissaten offer their customers special individual cups and saucers, sometimes appropriate to the type of coffee ordered, sometimes made in famous European porcelain factories.

Any visitor to Tokyo who is interested in the life-style of the Japanese, and possesses a leathery stomach, should explore the kissaten of either Harajuku or the Ochanomizu-Kanda area. The former are popular with schoolgirls, beautiful people and others of trendy disposition and are strong on pop music and radical interior design (names like *Move Café* and *Stardust*). The latter are full of university students. Slightly pretentious in a good-natured kind of way, many of them play classical music. A sharp pair of eyes are needed to spot the best coffee shops, which are often in basements or upper floors. Anyone just looking for a good cup of coffee will have no problem. Kissaten are everywhere. There are in the region of 130,000 of them in Tokyo.

Green tea is often served with Japanese food. It is never mixed with milk, sugar or lemon. It has a clean, fresh taste and an abundance of vitamin C, all of which are apparently too much for most pleasure-loving Japanese who drink *sake* or beer instead.

Sake is a clear, colourless, slightly sweet drink with about 16.5 percent to 17.5 percent alcohol content. It can be drunk hot, cold or with ice. It is made from fermented steamed white rice and yeast, to which malt and water are later added. There is a big difference between the good sake which is pure and the cheap varieties which are adulterated with alcohol and cane sugar. The latter, called *sanbaizoshu*, can leave the drinker with a nasty headache. The best sake is called *junmaishu*, and there are many different kinds. *Shochu* and *Awamori* are spirits distilled from grain. The taste is rough, not unlike that of Chinese spirits.

Beer is very popular in Japan and obtainable almost everywhere, including vending machines. Most of it is light and should appeal to Americans rather than Australians or Europeans. In recent years the public has favoured *nama* or draught beer rather than the ordinary variety. Most foreigners will probably like this as well as it does have more taste. However even a good beer like Sapporo Draught is made from rice and corn starch in addition to malt and hops, which is not exactly kosher (Purists who are en route to China should prefer the beer there.) The best imported brand that is widely available is Singapore-produced Heineken. Beer gardens are popular in the summer, where the refreshment is served with German-style food.

Many Japanese now drink wine, a revolutionary change in drinking habits of the past few years. The domestic product is heavily advertised and available in many coffee shops (which doesn't seem incongruous to the Japanese) and restaurants. Japanese wine however is only a little cheaper than imported, and the quality is never very high. The main producing area is Yamanashi Prefecture, on the north side of Mount Fuji.

Japanese talk a great deal about food, without much unanimity. Despite the difficulties involved in making definitions concerning Japanese food, there follows a list of the most typical kinds of eating and drinking establishments to be found in Japan. Japanese restaurateurs do not have to follow definitions, and visitors will sometimes encounter places that are half one thing and half another. The Japanese enjoy strange juxtapositions: the first entrepreneur to offer *sushi* with hot chocolate will probably make his fortune.

Eating and Drinking Houses

Rice Canteens

Shokudo

Rice canteens are the commonest, cheapest and shabbiest eating places to be found, but never the most unfriendly. The less sophisticated, the more remote the town, the more *shokudo* there are. Favoured by older people, the young disdain them for coffee shops. Canteens will sometimes have noren curtains outside, sometimes not. The thing to look for is a line of plastic models of rice dishes, covered with a layer of dust.

The Japanese are proud of the quality of their rice — heavier, richer and more sticky than Chinese or American varieties — and it is basic to the taste of their food. Foreigners find it easy to eat as the grains stick together and adhere to the chopsticks. (The Japanese *o-hashi* are short and square, much easier to use than the long, rounded Chinese chopsticks.)

The menu typically includes *donburi* bowls of rice topped with egg, meat or fish, *miso shiru* fermented bean paste soup, *ramen* 'Chinese' noodles, *gyoza* 'Chinese' *jiao-zi* dumplings, and such western favourites as *kare raisu* 'curry rice' (with Japanese pickles), *omuraisu* omelette stuffed with rice, potato croquettes and spaghetti. Flavoured syrup poured over shaved ice is served as a refreshment. Beer is always available, but not coffee.

'Eating Spots'

Shokuji-dokoro or *Meshiya*

Traditional Japanese food of a higher quality is served in very small restaurants called shokuji-dokoro. The menu is limited but contains more substantial meat and fish dishes than those available at rice canteens. Sake as well as beer is served.

Sake Houses

Izakaya or *Nomiya* or *Yakitoriya*

The classic sign of a sake house is a large red paper lantern, though some have white ones or even none at all. There are never any plastic models. Originally cheap and rather disreputable, there are now many smart ones that affect a rustic simplicity.

Sake houses have an equal emphasis on food and drink. Some offer a selection of the best sake, in the manner of a wine bar. They always have beer. Most have excellent food. It is served as a series of small, individually-ordered dishes. The menu is often on the wall. The most typical food is *yakitori* barbecued chicken. Grilled fish and squid are common as are *tofu* bean curd and *natto* fermented soy beans, but most sake houses have many other delicacies.

In a corner, either outside or inside there will often be a clay figure of a *tanuki*, the Japanese racoon dog, with a bottle of sake under his arm. A popular folk figure, the tanuki is a tricky, deceitful animal, but with a self-defeating weakness for the drink.

The atmosphere of a sake house is created by the person behind the counter, the *master* if he is a man, *mama-san* if she is a lady. Most of these places are very friendly and other customers will be pleased to have the opportunity of meeting foreigners. They may well pass over small bottles of sake.

Best visited in the evening, sake houses are easy to find and so small that good ones should only be recommended to close friends. One that is unusually large and very recommendable is located a few blocks behind the Kabuki Theatre in the Ginza: Chichibu Nishiki, 13-14 Ginza 2-chome, Chuo-ku, Tokyo, telephone (03) 541 4777.

Snack Bars

Sunakku Ba

Many 'western-style' bars serve snacks to avoid legal restrictions on places that only offer drinks. Often marked by purple signs illuminating girls' names, these places ply Japanese whisky rather than sake. Businessmen drown their frustrations and sorrows in the evenings, in the company of professional *mizu shobai* (water business) ladies who are expert listeners. The more expensive the drinks, the more congenial the companionship. These ladies would also offer their sympathy to foreign visitors, but unfortunately don't speak English.

Gourmet Restaurants

Ryoriya

Behind the noren there is another kind of restaurant, one that does not display plastic models of the food. From the outside some of them look like private homes or Japanese inns and can be very sophisticated. Prior reservations are often necessary and in some cases special personal introductions. The food is often served in private rooms.

Gourmet restaurants will usually specialize in the food of a particular locality (Kyoto cuisine is popular), a special style of cooking, or a certain kind of meat or fish. Vegetarian cuisine called *fucha ryori* or *shojin ryori* is sometimes prepared in these places.

The finest restaurants serve the sublime food associated with the tea ceremony called *kaiseki*. These special seasonal dishes originated in Kyoto. Imbued with Zen Buddhist simplicity, the cuisine paradoxically uses an enormous amount of paraphernalia. Guests are served a succession of small dishes arranged to the maximum aesthetic effect on valuable ceramic and lacquer vessels. Preparation is lengthy and the price for a *real* kaiseki dinner may well be ¥50,000 a head, *if* you have an introduction. Kaichi Tsuji, master of the famous Tsujitome restaurant in Tokyo, has written a book which is rather more palatable at US$42 (*Kaiseki, Zen Tastes in Japanese Cooking*, Kodansha International Tokyo and Palo Alto 1972).

Many of the more elegant speciality restaurants described below also qualify as gourmet restaurants.

Restaurants with Geisha Entertainers

Ryotei

Some particularly elegant places provide fine dinners during which the customers may if they wish be amused by *geisha*, Japan's traditional women entertainers. This is *extremely* expensive and foreign visitors would be advised to go only if they are accompanied by Japanese friends who will smooth the way for them.

Some evening tours include geisha performances and while these are not so authentic (and the food is inferior), the price should be quite bearable.

Speciality Restaurants
Soba Noodle Houses
Sobaya

Soba is the taste of the countryside of central and northeast Honshu. The noodles are made from buckwheat flour. Originally cheaper than rice, buckwheat was grown in mountainous areas with poor soil. Today soba noodles are no longer so cheap, but most dishes are still under Y1,000. Some soba houses are almost fashionable, but hopefully reservations will never become necessary.

The noodles can be eaten either hot or cold, or combined with other foods. *Tenzaru soba* is cold and served with deep-fried prawns and vegetables. The noodles are dipped in *tare* (a sauce made of *mirin* (a sweet spirit), bonito fish stock and soy sauce) to which onions and green *wasabi*, the Japanese horseradish, are added. After eating, some of the hot water used for cooking the noodles is added to the tare and the mixture is drunk as a final soup.

The best sobaya are in Yamagata (particularly the town of Obanazawa) and Nagano prefectures, but a list of good soba houses throughout Japan is available (in Japanese) in the magazine of the New Soba Association at the most famous soba address in Tokyo: Yabu Soba, 10 Kanda Awajicho 2-chome, Chiyoda-ku, Tokyo, telephone (03) 251 0287.

Udon Noodle Houses
Udonya

Thick white, almost-chewy wheat flour noodles called *udon* are preferred to soba in the Kansai area of Osaka, Kobe and Kyoto. They can be eaten either hot or cold, but ginger is often added to the tare dip rather than wasabi.

In summer, very fine wheat noodles called *somen* are served in iced water.

Ramen Shops
Ramenya

'Chinese soba' egg noodles are so cheap and so insipid that they are something of a national joke. But they are nevertheless popular and some visitors to Japan may even like them. The nutritional value compares well with potato crisps. Some of the shops describe themselves as 'Ramen Universities'.

Sushi Houses
Sushiya

The idea of raw fish only appeals to those who have eaten it. Conversion (like that of St Paul) is dramatic.

From the outside, sushi houses can usually be identified by the models in the window. Entering the restaurant, the customer has a choice of a seat at the counter, or at a side table. This is important. Sitting at the counter opposite the chef indicates that you intend to eat Tokyo-style *nigiri zushi*. These are pieces of fish, shellfish and other seafood on vinegared rice, conventionally ordered in pairs. (Pointing is easy enough.) The typical chef is very cheerful and talks continuously while he is preparing the food. Sushi should be eaten with the hands. The fish is dipped in soy sauce and eaten after invigorating the palate with pink pickled ginger. Green tea is served in thick, large cups.

Sitting at a side table, the customer has a choice of many other kinds of sushi. *Chirashi zushi* contains seafood arranged in a bowl over a bed of rice. *Maki zushi* are wrapped in seaweed. *Oshi zushi* are Osaka style. *Sashimi* is raw fish by itself, without rice.

Tokyo has the best sushi. The small restaurants near the Tsukiji Wholesale Fish Market have the freshest materials. (Small fishing ports and villages can be surprisingly disappointing.)

Eel Houses

Unagiya

Japanese chefs are unsurpassed when it comes to eel. The food is very popular and there are many restaurants specializing in *kabayaki*, barbecued eel covered with a thick, sweet soy-based sauce. The eel is sprinkled with a Japanese kind of pepper called *sansho*, and eaten with rice.

Blowfish Restaurants

Fugu Ryoriya

The *fugu* fish is an expensive and (slightly) dangerous delicacy. The liver and ovaries of the fish are toxic. However fugu chefs require a special licence to practise and only a few people are fatally poisoned each year. Japanese gourmands are fond of finely sliced raw blowfish, as well as a soup made from the left-overs. For health reasons the fish is best eaten between October and February. Some fugu restaurants display lanterns made from the dried skin of the fish.

Tempura Houses

Tempuraya

Adopted from the Portuguese in the 16th century, *tempura* is a style of deep frying seafood (especially prawns) and vegetables, covered in a light batter. Served hot (or it should be) the food is dipped in a mixture of fish stock, mirin, soy sauce and grated radish. There will usually be plastic models in the window.

Tonkatsu Houses

Tonkatsuya

Deep fried pork cutlet (fillet or boneless chops) was invented in Tokyo at the beginning of the century. It is served with a salad. There are always plastic models at the entrance of this kind of eating house. Tonkatsu is not expensive.

'Farmhouse' Restaurants

Robatayakiya or *Sumiyakiya*

Popular in the winter, these restaurants cook over a farmhouse-style fireplace or *irori*. The cook and his customers sit around the hearth, and he passes the grilled food across on a characteristic wooden board. The food is seasonal but will include fish, chicken, vegetables and bean curd.

Iron Hotplate Houses

Teppanyaki Ryoriya

Beefsteak, pork, seafood and vegetables are fried with a minimum of vegetable oil on iron hot plates (*teppan*). Expensive but deservedly popular with foreigners, this is also referred to as 'Genghis Khan' cooking (a fact which would have surprised the Great Khan and Scourge of the World).

Sukiyaki Houses

Sukiyakiya

Ever popular with tourists, *sukiyaki* (pronounced ski-yaki) is finely sliced beef cooked with vegetables, bean curd and *shirataki* (vegetable starch vermicelli), in soup stock containing soy sauce and *mirin*.

Shabu-shabu Restaurants

Shabu-shabu Ryoriya

Shabu-shabu has been adapted by the Japanese from the northern Chinese *Huoguo* (fire-pot) dish, also known as 'Mongolian Hotpot'. In China mutton is commonly used, but shabu shabu is beef. The meat is cooked with vegetables and bean curd in boiling water contained in a copper pot, and then dipped in a special sauce.

Oden Houses

Odenya

Oden is the cheap stew much loved by the Japanese, eaten in the winter. Bean curd, egg, vegetables, fishcake and a number of other things are boiled in a large copper cauldron is the middle of the restaurant. The cauldron is filled with a seaweed or fish-based stock to which soy sauce, sugar, and sake are added. The food is eaten with mustard. Not as common as some other kinds of restaurant, the best place to go is where the stew was invented: Nonki, 20-6 Mukogaoka 1-chome, Bunkyo-ku, Tokyo, telephone (03) 811-4736.

Other Restaurants

There are innumerable other speciality eating houses. *Chanko nabe* houses cook the substantial, body-building food associated with sumo wrestlers. *Mizutaki* restaurants offer a chicken version of sukiyaki. *Kamameshiya* steam a variety of foods in small clay pots. *Kushi age* houses have deep fried foods cooked on bamboo skewers.

There are some very fine restaurants specializing in crab, turtle and various kinds of fish. Some concentrate on chicken and other birds. Kyoto has some fantastically beautiful garden restaurants specializing in bean curd. There are a number of special places that serve traditional Japanese sweets.

Theatres and Railway Stations

Lunch boxes called *bento* were originally invented by caterers at kabuki theatres as a convenient way of selling cold food. *Maku-no-uchi bento*, 'between-the-acts lunch boxes', are now found in ordinary restaurants, but they are still served at the theatres.

In a later development the idea was taken up by railway stations, each one of which has its own special kind. These are called *eki-ben*. Famous eki-ben are sometimes on sale in department stores.

Street Food

On winter evenings the melancholy cry of the hot sweet-potato man ('*yaki imo*') can still be heard on the streets of the capital, though these days they use a *particularly* melancholy tape recording.

Ramen, oden and yakitori stalls are often found near railway stations. *Tako yaki*, made of batter with octopus and vegetable, is often sold on the street, also *okonomiyaki*, a savoury pancake filled with seafood, meat or vegetable that originates from Osaka.

Further Advice for the Gourmand Adventurer

There are two publications that should help the visitor who speaks little or no Japanese to do more than just look, point and nod. *Eating Cheap in Japan* (subtitled *The Gaijin Gourmet's Guide to Ordering in Non-tourist Restaurants*) by K Nagasawa and C Condon (Shufunotomo Company Limited, Tokyo 1972 ¥880) has colour photographs and descriptions of the most common Japanese dishes. The subtitle is more appropriate to the book than the title.

The JNTO publication called *The Tourists Handbook: Practical Ways to Relieve Your Language Problems* (recommended on page 123) also has useful pages on restaurant communication.

INDEX

A

accommodation 123
Adams, William 148
Ainu 7, 8, 9, 57, 112, 116
airlines 21
airports 20, 21
Aizu Basin 60
Akasaka 36, 49
Akihabara 28
Amanohashidate 92
angling 32
antiques 64
Aomori 64
archaeology 33
arts 33
Ashi, Lake 54
Aso, Mount 105
Asuka 80
audio equipment 28
Azusa, River 74

B

Bandai, Mount 60
banking 25
Basho 60
beer 114, 133
Beppu 110
bonsai 33
bookshops 28
Budda, statue of 52, 53
Buddhism 9, 12, 37, 53, 81, 85
Bullet Train 21, 68, 71, 92
bullfighting 103
bunraku 34, 89
buses 22
bushi 53

C

calligraphy 33, 85
car-hire 23

ceramics 85
cherry blossoms 15
Christianity 105
Chubu 65
Chugoku 93
Chuo line 22
cinema 34
climate 15
clothing 16
communications 24
crafts 28
credit cards 25
currency 25
cycling 32

D

Date, Masamune 60
deer park 81
department stores 27
disco 36
'Dome' 95
Donden, Mount 73
Dotombori 34
drink 130
driving licence 24
duty free 17

E

Edo 44, 45
Edo Period 88, 92
electrical appliances 28
electricity 17
entertainment 33

F

festivals (matsuri) 16, 37, 53, 86, 90, 117
film 17, 33, 34
flower arranging (ikebana) 33
food 130
Fuji, Mount 12, 15, 29, 54, 68
Fukuoka 21

G

geisha 36, 49, 88
geography 47
Ginza 36, 44, 49
Gion corner 33
Golden Week 16
Gold and Silver Pavilions 84
Goshogake 63

H

Hachimantai Plateau 63
Hagi 97
Hakodate 114
Hakone 54
Haneda Airport 21
Hayachine, Mt 63
health requirements 17
Hearn, Lafcadio 38
Hibiya Line 23
Hideyoshi 44, 56, 85, 89
Hiei, Mt 83
Higashima 60
Himeji 92
Hiraizumi 61
Hirayu Onsen 74
Hirosaki 64
Hiroshima 12, 95
history, periods in Japanese 13
history 44
Hokkaido 9, 12,, 15, 25, 115
Hongo 49
Honshu 12, 39, 57
horsemeat, raw 108
hot springs 16, 29, 32, 60, 63, 65, 75, 92, 108, 110
hotels 123

I

Ieyasu 44, 56, 71, 89
ikebana 33
ikebukuro 47, 51

imperial family 9
imperial palace 83
inns 123
Ise 77
Isuzu, river 77
Iwate, Mt 63
Izumo 97

J

Japan
  Airlines 21
  Alps 65, 73
  Automobile Federation 24
  Guide Association 20
  Hotel Association 125
  Mountaineering Association 29
  National Railways 21
  National Tourist Organization 123
  National Tourist Organization 17
  Traditional Craft Centre 28
  Travel Bureau 17, 20, 33
Jian Zhen 81
Jodogahama 63
Jomon people 8

K

kabuki 34, 45, 86
Kagoshima 12, 20, 108
Kamakura 52
Kamikochi 74
Kamo river 83
Kanazawa 21, 65, 71
Kanda 49
Kanda Jimbocho 28
Kansai 75, 77, 130
Kanto 39, 53, 130
Kasuga Shrine 81
Katsura 83
Kenroko garden 71
kimono 16, 17

Kinki 75
Kirishima, Mount 109
Kiso river 71
Kitakata 60
Kobe 90
Kochi 101
Kofukuji 81
Komorizuka Tomb 95
Konjikido mausoleum 61
Korea, influence of 8, 9
koto 33
Kumamoto 105
Kurashiki 93
Kyoto 9, 11, 13, 15, 52, 75, 80, 83
Kyushu 8, 12, 15, 20, 103

L

lacquerware 85
Leach, Bernard 57, 95

M

Maeda 71
martial arts 35
Marunouchi 44, 48
Mashiko 87
Matsue 97
Matsumoto 65, 73
matsuri (festivals) 37, 86, 90
Matsushima 58
Matsuyama 103
media 24
Meiji emperor 11, 45, 48, 60
    Restoration 11, 54, 75
Michinoku 57
Minamoto, Yoritomo 11, 53
    Yoshitsune 11, 53
Miyajima 95
Miyako 63
Miyazaki 109
Momoyama Period 85
money 25
Morioka 63

Motsuji 61
mountaineering 29
mountains 29, 65
museums 33, 48, 49, 71, 80, 85
music 36
Mutsu 65

N

Nagano prefecture 32
Nagasaki 103
Nagoya 20, 21, 65, 68
name cards 16
Nara 9, 11, 75, 78, 80, 81
national parks 29, 39, 61, 103, 109, 116
New Year 16
newspapers 24
nightlife 33, 36
Niigata 72
Nijo Castle 84
Nikko National Park 39
Nikko 11, 54
no theatre 34, 89
noodle houses 48
noren 130
Norikura, Mount 75
Noritake Company 71
Noto Peninsula 72

O

Obon festival 16
Okayama City 93
Okinawa 111
Omi Island 97
Omote Senke 33
orienteering 29
Osaka 16, 20, 34, 36, 75, 88
Osore, Mount 64
Otsu 20

P

pachinko 12, 81

Pacific Ocean coast 61
painting 33, 85
paperfolding (origami) 33
petrol 24
photographic equipment 27
population 44
post office 25
pottery 109
puppet theatre 89

R

radio 25
railway 48
recreation 29
Rikuchu Coast 61
Roppongi 36, 49, 51
ryokan 123

S

Sado Island 72
Sagami Bay 52
Saihitsuan Yuzen Silk Centre 71
sake 132, 134
Sakurajima 108
samurai 11, 53, 109
Sankeien 52
Sapporo 12, 21, 114
sculpture 85
Seibu 27
Sendai 58
Shibuya 47, 51
Shikoku 100
Shimokita Peninsula 64
Shimonseki 21
Shinkoku Island 12
Shinjuku Station 27
Shinto 9, 37, 77, 97, 98
shogun 11, 39, 44, 53
shopping 25
skiing 32
Soseki Natsume 103
sport 29

subway 22
sumo wrestling 35

T

Taisho era 92
Taito Island 50
Takamatsu 101
Takayama 75
Tamagawa 63
taxis 23
Tazawa, Lake 63
tea ceremony (chanoyu) 33, 63
tea 132
telegram 24
telephone 24
telex 24
temperatures 16
temples 48, 49, 50, 65, 71, 80
theatres 35, 49, 86
tipping 25
Tohoku 57, 58
Tokugawa 11, 39, 45, 48, 54, 56, 60
Tokushima 101
Tokyo Journal 37
Tokyo 11, 12, 15, 16, 20, 24, 37, 41-51
Tourist Information Centres 20, 28, 33, 37
Towada, Lake 63
Trans-Siberian Railway 21
transport 20
Tsugaro Peninsula 64
Tsukiji 49
Tsushima Island 8

U

Uji River 83
ukiyo-e 45
Ura Senke Tea School 33

V

visas 17

W

Wajima 72
Warner, Langdon 80
Weston, Walter 74
Wild Bird Society of Japan 32
wildlife 32

Y

Yamanote Line 221
Yamato Plain 78, 80
Yayoi 8, 9
yen 25
Yokohama 20, 21, 22, 52
yukata 16

Z

Zen monasteries 84